WHY I AM
A JEW

By David de Sola Pool

Portraits Etched in Stone, 1952

An Old Faith in the New World, 1955
(With Tamar de Sola Pool)

WHY I AM A JEW

By

David de Sola Pool

BEACON PRESS   BOSTON

To Tamar, my wife,
daughter of a long line of rabbis,
co-author of this book,
our humble tribute
to the heritage we cherish

FOREWORD

THIS BOOK tries to tell why I am a Jew and why I rejoice to
be one. It might have been written in a far more personal
vein. It might have passed in review more than three score
years and ten from childhood and youth in a home where
Jewish traditions were as natural as the air that was breathed,
to the years of study under masters of thought and learning
in several countries, and to the half century of my ministry
under the benign roof of Shearith Israel synagogue of America's oldest Jewish congregation. I could have touched on
intimate views of varied communities the world over, or
dwelt on endeavors to give service to Jewish men in the
armed forces, and on personal participation in the rebirth of
Zion and the rebuilding of the Land of Israel. The story of
these and many other personal experiences would have run
over the bounds of a small volume and perhaps have gone
beyond its purpose. But were this book more personal or
even more impersonal than it is, it would have made little
difference, for I can draw no dividing line between my
faith and my life.

The traditions in which I am rooted had their origin
in the Holy Land. Yet they live vibrantly in the four corners
of the earth. American Jewish soldiers observing the Passover in Arctic Thule, Jews reading their Hebrew prayers in

Central Africa or South America, or others translating their scriptures into Maharathi in Bombay, Tamil in Cochin, Arabic in the Near East, or medieval Spanish in Turkey, are all alike part of the Jewish people.

The story of the Jew even as it embraces the wide distances also transcends time. Judaism is ancient and modern, a continuity of four thousand years. With its emphasis on the future, it has no final stopping place. It cannot be described or defined only dogmatically in terms of theology, for it is a comprehensive philosophy which penetrates every aspect of living. It demands of its adherents study and knowledge, the hallmark of Jewish life. Since these are grounded in the Bible, they are more than an intellectual storing of the mind. They are the formative discipline and the enrichment of mind, heart and soul, and they partake of the Infinite from which they are derived. Knowledge of Judaism can never be static. The reading in the synagogue of the Five Books of Moses in consecutive portions every Sabbath in the year, the illuminating selections from the prophetic and historical books, the daily recital of Psalms, are not mere repetitions. Each engenders new understanding and reveals new light. A man cannot attain to the end of the message of the Bible, however high he may lift his gaze, however deeply he may probe. The Torah, and the Synagogue which is both the House of Study and the House of Worship, have assured the preservation of the Jew and of his faith.

It is the whole of the time-tested tradition that has been pivotal in the survival of the Jewish people through the ages. It is this which has united each Jew with his ancestors from Bible days. And it is this which wherever he may be organically relates him with all whom men regard as Jews. His being a Jew is a synthesis of religious, historic, cultural and emotional consciousness that transcends all diversities within the people, theological, philosophic, demographic, linguistic, or geographic.

I offer this small book humbly, as a sheaf garnered from the rich harvest of Judaism. A massive literature, a history of four thousand years, a courageous, articulate and unending struggle for moral determinism, cannot readily be compressed, nor would I make bold to attempt to do this without the earnest hope that this book may be but an introduction to the study of the great tradition which it is our heritage to know, to understand and to share.

D. DE SOLA POOL

New York, N. Y.

CONTENTS

ONE

TO BE A JEW

WHY I AM A JEW—If this be a question, the simplest answer is that my mother and my father were Jews. But one is a Jew not only because of the accident of birth, analogously to having red hair like mother or a broad physique like father. The will to be a Jew involves more than being the child of Jewish parents. One may equally well ask why they were Jews, and their parents before them, and all the generations before them, far back into the beginnings of recorded history. The question is of our time; the answer comes from of old.

Among my earliest memories are those of pictures on the walls of my home. One was of a great-great-grandfather, Raphael Meldola, a chief rabbi of Anglo-Jewry. Another was of a great-grandfather, D. A. de Sola. He had edited and translated from Hebrew into English the prayerbooks used in our home and in our synagogue. His lineage has been traced back to the ninth century, and on that family tree there are in many generations rabbis whose names and writings are known. But as a Jew I can look much farther than that. Indeed, I think back four thousand years and

13

muse on why and how my ancestors have maintained their
Jewish selves throughout all these generations.

This continuity of Jewish life is dramatically illustrated by
the posterity of the ancient priesthood. Every Mr. Cohen is
directly descended in the male line for some thirty-two
centuries from Aaron, the brother of Moses. Similarly, every
Mr. Levy or Mr. Levin comes in unbroken line from Levi,
the third son of Abraham's grandson, the patriarch Jacob.
The Abarbanel family preserves a tradition of centuries
that they stem from King David. The Jewish people as a
whole honors and cherishes the continuity of its historic
memories of a hundred generations on which the founding
fathers, Abraham, Isaac, and Jacob, have set their indelible
patriarchal stamp. There is no claim to descent from demi-
gods, from mythological heroes, or from eponymous super-
men. Any attempt to impress upon the consciousness of the
Jewish people an arrogant, vainglorious, or even romantic
idealizing of the past would be quickly dispelled by reference
to the Bible.

Of itself, length of ancestry warrants no claim to aristocracy. All men alike descend from countless generations. It is
true that there is in the Hebrew Bible great stress on pedigree.
When Moses and Aaron gathered the people in the wilder-
ness in order to take a census, it was not just numbers that
they were compiling. "They assembled all the community
together and they declared their descent after their families,
by their fathers' houses, according to the number of names"
(Numbers 1:18). In many a chapter the Bible lists names
of who begat whom. But for all the emphatic insistence on
knowing who he is and whence he has sprung, the Jew is
never allowed to forget that his first known ancestors were
shepherds, and their descendants slaves in Egypt. When in
Bible days he brought to the Temple his offering of first fruits
of his harvest, his declaration of thankfulness began by

recalling that his ancestors were Bedouin, wandering, homeless Syrians (Deuteronomy 26:5). The uncompromising realistic frankness of the Biblical narratives does not permit any fanciful distortions of his origin, however well meant. The burning words of the Biblical prophets with their unsparing denunciation of corruptions among their people have never been censored, suppressed, or explained away. They have been accepted by all the generations which hearkened and constantly reread their challenging truths. While the Bible story never glosses over weaknesses in the people and frankly tells of their defections, such as in the worship of the golden calf at the very foot of Mount Sinai, it also recalls their glory. It was they who received, preserved and gave to the world the Ten Commandments, the immortal teachings of the prophets, and the world's highest social and moral ideals.

During the journeying through the centuries many groups and individuals were lost and disappeared from the path of Jewish tradition. At one time nearly two thousand seven hundred years ago no less than ten out of the twelve Jewish tribes were wiped out by military conquest. At that time it was a theme of the prophet Isaiah that of the remaining two tribes, only a remnant would surely endure. In every generation were those whose evaluation of their unique spiritual and moral inheritance and their loyalty to it assured the survival of at least a saving remnant of the people of Israel.

Twenty-four hundred years ago in Persia there arose a malevolent Haman who sought utterly to destroy the Jewish people. Between him and the sadistically crazed Hitler, many a bigoted tyrant has arisen to vilify and persecute the Jew. His existence today despite his suffering makes a challenging phenomenon of his survival and his will to live on. There is an old saw that it is not easy to be a Jew. Even in free lands where a man's right to live his faith is not questioned, it presents problems to remain members of a minority. Yet Jews feel a deep compulsion to transmit their demanding heritage to the generations to come. Many there are who ask the question why.

In countries such as the United States of America they enjoy the right and freedom to be themselves. Their religious liberty is guaranteed by the Constitution and separation of Church and State. They mingle freely with their neighbors of other faiths. Yet it is often anything but easy for the Jew to maintain himself as a Jew. Being a member of the Jewish group involves setting on himself and on his family difficult and sometimes sacrificial obligations. Most of the world around him goes not to synagogue but to church. It treats his seventh-day Sabbath of rest as a working day. It celebrates Easter while he is observing his Passover. When he is kindling the lights of his festival of Hanukkah, every one else is lighting a Christmas tree. In other lands in dark hours of Jewish history, riot, plunder and massacre have been not unknown accompaniments of differences in calendar such as these. None the less, even in the absence of danger or violence, and in a social background that may be friendly and understanding, there are difficulties of adjustment in the preservation of Jewish individuality in a predominantly non-Jewish environment. Why, then, do I still wish to be a Jew?

The primary answer is given by history. It is ancestral traditions from the past, a distinctive historic consciousness today, and a consecrated purpose for the future which give the Jew strength to persist, and which unite and preserve the Jewish people.

Some eight hundred years ago the brilliant Spanish Jewish physician, poet, and philosopher, Jehudah Halevi, wrote a work based on the historic conversion to Judaism of the Khazars of South Russia. He imaginatively told how the

king of the Khazars, seeking for a new religion, summoned
representative spokesmen to set forth their doctrines before
him. First, the philosopher-scientist, then the Christian, and
then the Moslem defined themselves in terms of their beliefs.
The Jew began to define himself to the king in terms of
his history. What makes a Jew is history no less than doctrine.
We needs must tell something of our story to explain why we
are Jews.

But before the curtain is lifted on our past, we must understand what we mean by the term Jew.

TWO

WHAT IS A JEW?

WHAT IS A JEW? What has gone into the making of the Jew?

A century ago Count Gobineau published his four-volume essay on racial inequalities among mankind. He and his followers created the concepts of the legendary Nordic Aryan as a synonym of noble civilization, in contrast with the Semite and other supposedly well-defined racial groups. Are Jews members of a distinctive race?

We need not here attempt to give an exact definition of the scientifically loose and blurred term, race. In the sociological sense Jews form a distinctive group with a consciousness of their group characteristics, and with a certain recognized collective identity. This is not something that is due simply to racial inheritance. We cannot with scientific precision label the Jew as a Semite by race, for the word Semite like the word Aryan is primarily a linguistic term.

The Bible leaves us no doubts as to the fact that of old there were not a few racial admixtures in the Jewish people. This began most markedly when a mixed multitude joined the children of Israel in their exodus from Egypt. The prophet Ezekiel even dared to say (15:3), "Your origin and your birth are of the land of the Canaanites. The Amorite was your father and your mother a Hittite." These were two very different racial types. The Amorite was blond, yellow-skinned and blue-eyed, while the Hittite was swarthy, with oblique eyes and high cheek bones. Since Biblical days, migrations, conversions to Judaism, environmental influences, and a small measure of marital interpenetration from the peoples among whom the Jews lived, have created Jewish ethnic agglomerations of the most varied physical types. Among Jews one may find men with widely differing shape of skull, extending from the long headed (dolichocephalic) to the broad headed (brachycephalic) type. They have noses of every shape. The often caricatured hooked nose is seen on ancient sculptures of Hittites, and it marked the faces of men such as Emerson, the Duke of Wellington, and Cardinal Newman. Anthropologists tell us that among Jews it is found in only one of every seven. The nose most frequently seen on the face of a Jew is the straight Greek nose. In stature, color of skin, and every other physical feature the most varied types are found among Jews. They range from the blond Germanic through the darker Mediterranean types, to the swarthy South Arabian Yemenites and the black African Falashas, or the black Jews of Cochin and the Bnai Israel in India. It is biologically inevitable that those who have lived for centuries in South Arabia under the influences of its sun, its climate, its diet, its culture, its social standards, and all the other factors affecting bodily type, should have developed physical variations from those who for centuries have lived in a Northern European milieu with altogether other environmental conditions. Mr. Cohen and Mr. Levy, who, as we have seen, are unquestionably descended directly from Jews of the earliest Bible days, as a rule are in their general physical type one with their environment whether it be Northern or Southern, Eastern or Western.

Clearly one is not a Jew by race. What then is the meaning of the term, a designation that occurs for the first time in the Biblical book of Jeremiah (34:9)?

It is not a political appellation. A citizen of the reborn Jewish nation in the land of Israel today is an Israeli, and he may be a member of any racial group or religion. Nor is the term identified with any single localized geographical grouping. Jewish selfhood is unique. It involves affiliation with a distinctive religious brotherhood which at the same time integrates one into a distinctive people. It is characterized not only by religion, as is being a Buddhist, Christian or Moslem. It is also a cultural entity, an idea made flesh, a physical embodiment of a distinctive soul born of Judaism.

In Jewish law a Jew is regarded as one until he makes personal renunciation of his Jewish allegiance by joining another religion. On the other hand, anyone from whatsoever grouping he may derive, who accepts Judaism as his religion thereby becomes a Jew and at the same time shares in the collective identity of the Jewish people. Entrance into the fold is automatic with the acceptance of Judaism, just as leaving the fold is automatic through acceptance of another faith.

Friedrich Wilhelm, the King of Prussia, once asked his chaplain to prove in one word the verity of religion. "Your majesty," the chaplain replied, "the Jews." The Jew is the embodiment of a long and continuous history of religious ideas and teachings for which he has struggled actively and passively to gain world recognition through the ages. Goethe could say of the Jewish people, "In independence, steadfastness and valor, and when all this would prove insufficient, in tenacity, it has no match. It is the most persevering nation

in the world. It is, it was, and it will be to glorify the name
of God throughout all time."

In all the centuries of their dispersion they as a rule spoke
the language of the land where they dwelt. They were
subject to all the diverse influences of their cultural environment. Yet largely because of their distinguishing religious
regulations, as well as in a measure because of centuries of
physical isolation often violently enforced from without
as during the dark Middle Ages, they maintained their own
distinctive character throughout their long annals. "Remember the days of old, consider the years of many generations"
(Deuteronomy 32:7). If we are to understand more fully
what has produced and preserved their identity and con
tinous determined will for survival, we must look back over
the whole of their chronicles. This begins with the Bible,
the *Biblion, the* book. It was the Jew who made the Bible,
and it has been the Bible which has made the Jew.

THREE

THE FIRST TWO THOUSAND YEARS

THE BIBLE is in reality not one book. It is an ancient library of thirty-six books of prose, poetry, laws, history, archives, oratory, philosophy, hymns, songs, dirges, drama, proverbs, riddles, correspondence, diaries, idylls. Its opening keynote chapters tell nothing of the story of the Jew. They are dedicated to an interpretation of the beginnings of mankind. They tell about not a man named Adam, but about Ha-Adam, man, who is declared to be created in the image of God. The first eleven chapters continue in this universalist context the beginnings of man's story on earth. We are thus prepared for the momentous revelation that came to Abraham that there is the one and only one God. The rabbis frequently state that until the time of Abraham God was the God only of the heavens. But through Abraham and his Jewish descendants He became what the Bible calls "the God of the heavens and the God of the earth" (Genesis 24:3). Thus monotheism was born.

Abraham grew up in a world in which his father and all around him worshiped the sun god, the moon god, the god of pestilence, and a host of other often malign gods and demons which had to be appeased by practises of dark magic. His vision of monotheism was more than a negation of that world. It was a positive revelation. His proclamation of one universal God was the farthest reaching and most comprehensive of all spiritual truths. There is but one God of all mankind, not a god for every little local people splitting men up into jealous warring groups, but one God drawing all men together in unity of brotherhood, all alike His children. In the spirit of the opening words of the Bible, "In the beginning God created the heavens and the earth," Abraham realized and proclaimed that there is only one God whose spirit can be felt and recognized in every phenomenon and in every experience that man may know.

With this basic teaching of the one God, all life takes on unity of purpose and can become a profoundly spiritual experience. Man need never be left in darkness, for the light of God can be his guide from birth to death. Judaism sees in the great mechanism of the universe a manifestation of God in an ordered creation bound together by one cosmic law. In all the infinite variety of nature, He is the one First Cause, the one creative force, the one universal intelligence governing all existence. Human life is not given over to blind chance or disorderly competing polytheisms. Man is not hopeless and friendless, a tiny insignificant mote in a relentless and soulless cosmos. There is the one God who unifies all creation, who is the ultimate spirit of all that exists, who brings unity and harmony into all the multiplicity of experience, who resolves all the discords of life, and who speaks to the very heart of man. Man is not a victim caught between the forces of good and evil, between God and the devil. There is but one force, one power, one dominion—the one God.

According to Jewish tradition, patriarch Abraham sought to bring this vision to the people among whom he lived.

When he left the northland to settle in Canaan, he went with Sarai, his wife, his nephew Lot, "and the souls which they had made in Haran" (Genesis 12:5). These words are interpreted as referring not to children of their body but to the souls they had won over to their recognition of God. The religion of Abraham opened new vistas in man's spiritual development. It was a summons to mankind to rise above degrading worship of ignoble mumbo-jumbo gods and goddesses which had to be placated by sorcerers. It called on men to turn away from Baal and Ashtoreth, cruel nature gods and loathsome sexual monsters. It bade mankind give up orgiastic lascivious rites and debauchery within its temples and on every high hill and under every green tree. It appealed to men to rise above the concept of mean gods and goddesses such as later won wide recognition in the ancient Greek or Roman pantheon. These man-made deities were formed in the flawed and warped image of their human creators. They were characterized by all the petty jealousies and unsparing cruelties, dishonesties and lusts which thwarted men on earth. They were conceived of as gods who would arbitrarily and capriciously intrude into human affairs to protect a favored warrior, or wreak their spite against a man who had incurred their personal enmity. A Prometheus who brought the heavenly fire to earth was murdered by the jealous gods. They hurled down to destruction Icarus who flew high towards the heavens. It was Abraham, the first Jew, who with God's blessing soared beyond such teaching as those of a god who shares his power with animal gods and trumpery godlings. He began to lift man's faith beyond a religion such as that of ancient Egypt with its opposing gods of light and darkness, and of abundance and want, or the religion of later Persia with an Ormuzd, the supreme creator of all good, and Ahriman, the supreme creator of all evil, in perpetual conflict with each other.

Monotheism lifted mankind above mind-darkening and soul-blinding beliefs in demons, evil spirits, witchcraft, and every kind of superstition, and repudiated the attribution of divinity to men and monarchs.

To all who would hear, it proclaimed the teaching of the sacredness of human life. In the story of the attempted sacrifice of his son Isaac (Genesis 22) Abraham dramatically learned that men must no longer practise in the name of religion the brutalities and inhuman horror sanctified by the peoples among whom he lived. They burned children alive in sacrifice to Moloch, or would seal a living child in the cornerstone of a new building to placate the gods. It was his vision which eventually triumphed over such horrors and the heartless casting out of unwanted infants widely practised by ancient peoples. The Book of Psalms (47:10) calls the Jewish people "the people of the God of Abraham." One who joins their faith is designated as "a child of Abraham our father." Since his time, nearly four thousand years ago, the spiritual children of Abraham have been protestants against superstitions and social evils. Here is the primary reason why I am and why I wish to remain a Jew, the heir of a supreme spiritual mission going back to my ancestor Abraham and still needed by all mankind.

The revelation which came to Abraham was but the beginning of a purposive existence for his people through all the subsequent generations. Of him God said: "I have known him to the end that he may command his children and his household after him to keep the way of the Lord to do righteousness and justice," "and all the nations of the earth shall bless themselves by him" (Genesis 18:17, 18). Some six centuries later, Moses in Egypt lived in a land where religion expressed a groping fear of many gods such as the sun and the moon, a highly developed cult of death with the Book of the Dead as a sacred text, and the elaborate religious

rituals of mummification, worship of animals such as Apis
the bull, the crocodile, the dog, the cat, the falcon, and the
ape. It was a land where slavery of man's body and soul was
an accepted social practise. After looking upon the burdens
of the downtrodden children of Israel, Moses threw in his
lot with the enthralled sufferers. From that moment he ceased
to be a comfortable gentleman of the royal palace whose life
might not have caused a ripple on the surface of world
history. Pharaoh was an absolute monarch venerated as a god,
but Moses stood firm against the question hurled at him by
Pharaoh (Exodus 5:2), a question that has so often been
directed to the Jew, "Who is the Lord that I should hearken
to His voice?"

For Moses religion was the very opposite of an opiate for
the masses. It was shot through with revolutionary and far-
visioned practical measures looking toward emancipation from
miseries born of indigence, crushing toil, slavery, and the
eclipse of hope. "You shall remember that you were slaves
in Egypt" runs through the Pentateuch of Moses as a refrain
which motivates the observance of the Sabbath and festivals
as days of happiness and rest from toil, and which inspires
such social injunctions as those of loving the stranger, not
oppressing the poor, not exacting interest from him nor
taking the widow's garment in pledge, leaving part of the
harvest for the poor, not perverting justice for one's fellow
men, and having true and honest balances, weights and
measures (Deuteronomy 5:15; 15:15; 10:19; 24:22. Leviticus
19:34, 36, 25:38, 42, 55). This social definition of religion,
first recorded by Moses, became the world's primary motive
power working for mankind's life, liberty, and the pursuit of
happiness.

In the eyes of Heinrich Heine the stature of Moses dwarfs
Mount Sinai itself. For "unlike the Egyptians he did not
shape his works of art out of brick and granite. He built

pyramids of men and carved obelisks out of human material. He took a poor shepherd tribe and transformed it into a people destined to outlive the centuries . . . He created Israel." Under the leadership of Moses this came to pass through the exodus from Egypt and the revelation at Mount Sinai.

In a well-know parable the rabbis pictured God as desiring to give the Ten Commandments to all men on earth. He offered them, they said, to the descendants of Esau. They cautiously asked, "What is in them?" When they heard the words "Thou shalt not kill," they said, "We cannot accept them, for our ancestor said of us, 'By your sword you shall live' " (Genesis 27:10). God then offered them to the descendants of Lot. They also asked, "What is in them?" When they heard the words "Thou shalt not commit adultery," they replied, "We cannot accept them, for we have sprung from such relationships." Thereupon He offered them to the descendants of Ishmael. In their turn they asked, "What is in them?" and they were told, "Thou shalt not steal." They answered, "We cannot accept these laws, for of us it was said that 'his hand should be against everyone' " (Genesis 16:12). God finally offered them to the children of Israel. They asked what is in them, and they were told that they implied not only the ten but six hundred and thirteen commandments. Their immediate answer was "All that the Lord our God may speak . . . we shall hear and do" (Deuteronomy 5:24).

In vivid fancy the rabbis say that when God gave the Ten Commandments to the Jews, every word proclaimed was echoed simultaneously in all the seventy languages of the earth, that all men might hear and make those words their own. Moreover, the commandments were given in the desert and not in the land of the children of Israel, so that the Jewish people could not say that they were given to them alone as their own national possession. The revelation at Mount Sinai gave them to all the world, for they are addressed in the singular as though to every human being on earth individually.

Explicitly and implicitly bound up with them are all the other soul-building rules of the Torah. This word designating primarily the five books of Moses means direction, guidance, teaching, instruction. It is often translated inadequately as law. The Torah sets up the organization for a commonwealth with human liberty under law.

The Torah of Moses is the Magna Carta of mankind. Centuries before Plato's Republic was written, the social code of the Torah set up a blueprint of an ideal commonwealth. It is permeated with a passion for social justice and human rights. It lays less stress on the pious self-centered quest of personal salvation than on building a just and enlightened human society. In a world strangely indifferent to such values, it emphasizes social concern with restrictions on capitalism. It prohibits the outright selling and permanent alienation of one's patrimony lest that result in an uprooted and impoverished landless peasantry. It sees no virtue or saintliness in poverty and in refusing to enjoy the gifts which God makes available to man. Life's blessings are not to be renounced but to be developed by work and to be enjoyed.

A rabbi loved to tell that when Ha-Adam, the man in the Elysian Garden of Eden, heard the words of his punishment that henceforth the soil would bring forth thorns and thistles, his eyes filled with tears, and he turned toward the heavenly voice and said, "Must I and my ass eat from the same manger?" But when he heard the heavenly voice continue with the words, "By the sweat of your brow you shall eat bread," he was comforted. The Torah sets up labor as an explicit command incumbent on rich and poor alike, but it limits work to six days in the week. Then it enunciates a principle unique in its time when men plodded in unbroken toil day after day. It proclaims that after six days of work the seventh day that follows shall be a Sabbath for all. In the Ten Commandments given at Mount Sinai the days of work are regulated equally for the weary laborer and for the employer of labor. Einstein was impressed by the fact that in the commandment to keep the Sabbath holy, the animals were also expressly included, thus setting forth as an ideal the demand for the solidarity of all living things. Far more strongly yet is expressed the demand for the solidarity of humankind.

The world-challenging social standards set up for the first time in man's history by the Torah of Moses are revealed not in the name of a remote god uninterested in human welfare, but in the name of a God who in His opening words at Mount Sinai declared Himself to be "the Lord your God who brought you out of the land of Egypt out of the house of bondage" (Exodus 20:2).

The Torah of Moses does not make religion the province of an ecclesiastical hierarchy, and social justice the domain of secular courts and political government. In Judaism law is not divorced from but is an expression of religion. The Torah gives the organically united authority of both religion and society to the requirement of compulsory care of the widow, the orphan, the poor, the sick, and the stranger. It ordains that each seventh year shall be a year of agricultural rest for the land with all the earth's produce made freely available to the poor. The fiftieth year which is the year of jubilee becomes the signal for the proclamation of freedom for all contract laborers, and for all servants to return to their family inheritance. In that year also a patrimony of land which one has leased to another reverts in absolute possession to the original owner or to his heirs.

Such unique legislation aims to overcome lasting poverty

and to make impossible the growth of large landed estates in the hands of a few. The Torah of Moses outlines the setting up of a society in which there will be no privileged class of wealthy aristocrats and no hereditary oligarchy enjoying special prerogatives and immunities. This revelation of society organized on the basis of an all-pervasive justice was given to the people as a whole. Thereby the masses of the commonalty become a people of aristocrats before God. The Torah, the basic code of Judaism throughout the ages, uniquely combines the spiritual aspirations of the individual with social and national practical ideals many of which our world of today has yet to learn.

These expressions of social idealism no less than the unique theology were the more amazing to an uncomprehending world because they were not born of fear. They are pervaded by a sense of awe before God, and even more are they infused by God's love of man and man's love of God and love of his neighbor. Hillel, great rabbinic luminary who lived in the century preceding the Christian era, was challenged by a heathen sceptic to teach him the whole of Judaism while standing on one foot. In reply, Hillel reformulated the Golden Rule that he knew from the Torah (Leviticus 19:18), "You shall love your neighbor as yourself," and said, "What is hateful to you, do not do to your fellow man. That," said Hillel, "is the sum of all Jewish teaching. Now go and learn its parts."

Judaism is not expressed by easy verbal assent to certain supernal principles. It calls for a regimen of living that translates their application to life. What of the Torah of Moses would have been preserved for the world had the Jews been limited to generalized ideals, instead of being trained by specific laws, rules, regulations and practises, is not an altogether unanswerable question. Josephus (38–100 C. E.) pointed out that whereas the philosophers of his

day addressed themselves to a few select companions and
disciples, Moses gave his teaching to his whole people in the
form of ceremonials.

The excellence of the laws of the Torah is no assured
guarantee of their observance. In ancient days disregard of
them called forth the most impassioned, the most glowing,
and the most intensely moral oratory that man has ever
heard. In tones which reecho around the world today the
Biblical prophets appealed for justice and brotherly love,
the two cardinal principles which complement each other
and together characterize the legislation of the Torah. It was
the prophets who taught that the essence of true religion is
expressed through love of neighbor conjoined with the
practise of righteousness.

Who were these prophets?

The word prophet as a translation of the Hebrew term
nabi is sometimes misleading. Nabi means one who proclaims.
The nabi was primarily not a foreteller but a forthteller, not
a soothsayer but a truthsayer. He is also called a *roeh*, a seer,
one who has a vision of the Divine. He spoke because of an
irresistible call within his soul. At times he may have
fervently desired to hold back the inspired words the utterance of which could endanger his life. When the prophet
Jeremiah wished to keep silent, he could not, and he cried
out, "If I say I will not make mention of Him nor speak
any more in His name, then there is in my heart as it were
a burning fire shut up in my bones, and I weary myself to
hold it in, but I cannot" (20:9). Jonah tried to flee to the
far ends of the earth to escape the burden of his mission to
Nineveh and the utterance of the daring imperilling words
aflame within him. But he was forced to learn that the
prophet cannot withhold the message it is his to proclaim.
The prophets were the mentors of kings, princes, commoners
and priests alike. They were the vocal conscience of their

people, excoriating the demoralization and evils of their day, and indeed of our day.

Sometimes, as with Amos, the herdsman and dresser of sycamore trees, the burden of the prophet's message is a fearless and impassioned denunciation of depravity, self-indulgence and injustice in high places, and a calling for justice and rights for the masses. "Hate the evil and love the good, and establish justice in the gate . . . Let justice roll down as waters, and true justice as a never failing stream" (Amos 5:15, 24). Sometimes as with Hosea, the emphasis is on the need for a forgiving tenderness and love. Sometimes, as with Habakkuk, the prophet fearlessly questions why the good often suffer and the wicked often prosper. The answer he gives is that the righteous lives by his faith (2:4). Sometimes the prophet gives a classical summation of the need for sincerity in the conventional forms of religion, as when Joel (2:13) bids the people rend their heart and not their garments. Sometimes the prophet echoes the call for the true standards of living as did Zechariah (4:6) after he heard the divine word that life must be guided not by might, nor by power, but by the spirit of God. Also the prophet Jeremiah (9:22, 23) proclaimed God's word that the wise should not glory in his wisdom, nor the strong in his might, nor the rich in his wealth, but man should glory in understanding and knowing God who exercises mercy, justice and righteousness on earth, for it is in these things that God delights.

It should be clearly recognized that the prophets were not opposed to the ritual of the Temple; but when an offering was brought as a substitute for moral living, they regarded it as a subversion of the law. They taught that when ritual is not conjoined with God-revering conduct it is a vain plaster over a festering sore. They insist that no ritual or sacrificial offerings can take the place of the good life. The prophet Samuel, who repeatedly offered ritual sacrifices, de-

clares (I Samuel 15:22) that to obey God is better than
sacrifice. Micah maintains (6:6–8) that religion is not attested
by the number of offerings that one might bring to the
altar; it must express itself by doing justly, loving mercy, and
walking in purity with God. Similarly Isaiah sternly proclaims the word of God that sacrifices and trampling the
courts of the Temple are an abomination when they are
conjoined with evil living, that God hates and He is weary of
bearing with the celebration of Sabbath and religious festivals
when these go together with iniquity. God cannot abide
hands stretched out in prayer when the hands are full of
blood. What God asks of us for any ritual to be acceptable
to Him is, the prophet asserts, "Wash yourselves, make yourselves clean; put away the evil of your doings from before
My eyes; cease to do evil, learn to do good; seek justice,
relieve the oppressed; defend the fatherless, plead for the
widow" (1:11–17).

While the message of the prophets was directed primarily
to their own people, they had the vision of humanity as a
whole, and many of their words were addressed to other
nations. Bearers of a world message, they called on all men
of their day and of the generations to come to hearken to
the God of all mankind. They were the first true inter-
nationalists. They summoned Gentile and Jew alike to infuse
both individual and social life with true moral and religious
motivation, and so build on earth the Kingdom of God
when all mankind shall live at peace.

The Hebrew prophets are indeed a unique phenomenon
in history. Their words, sacredly treasured by the very people
whom they excoriated, have been for the world watchwords of
moral progress. To this day the Jew regards it as one of the
main purposes of his survival to preserve and repeat the
message of the prophets, so desperately needed for the upbuilding of our troubled world.

The last recorded word heard by the last of the prophets (Malachi 3:22) "Remember the Torah of Moses My servant which I commanded him in Horeb for all Israel," constitute a dramatic reminder of the basis of Judaism. Yet the Torah of Moses was never regarded as a static, finalized revelation. During all the centuries of the Biblical period it was subject to interpretation and organic development. The flaming words of the prophets are one expression of this. Another is to be found in the Book of Psalms to which the Jewish and the Christian world give devout acclaim.

What the prophet aimed to do for the community of men, bringing them closer to God through righteous living, the Psalmist sought to do for the individual soul through identification with the divine.

Over the centuries the Psalms have become a household treasury no less than a cardinal part of the synagogue service. They have given uplift and strength to the Jew and to the Christian also in every aspect of their inner life. They have helped overcome sin by rapt self-purification. They have conquered discouragement through strengthening hope. They have triumphed over sorrow by sanctifying joy. They have surmounted doubt through their aspiring faith. For the Jew the Psalms have potently expressed the religious idealism which inspirit the regulations and ritual of the Torah, just as for his forebears they expressed the spiritual uplift of the Temple's ritual services.

The Torah, the prophets, and the Psalms constitute a major part of the Biblical message to the world. But there are also the Bible's historical books which depict a political advance characterized by the struggle for recognition of the supreme concept of the God of Abraham and of Moses. Three other books in the Hebrew Bible, Proverbs, Job, and Ecclesiastes, reinforce the teaching of Judaism that brave thinking must save man from either unrealistic, doctrinaire, categorical optimism, or hopeless, fatalistic pessimism.

Ancient Greeks gave birth to science by delving into physical phenomena, and to philosophy by their speculations about the nature of the universe. The Jew with his Bible began with a revealed knowledge of the one universal God as the First Cause. By applying this to all phenomena he gave birth not to an abstract intellectual philosophy, but to an ethical and spiritual interpretation of every aspect of life. For the Jew, wisdom has a moral connotation alongside the intellectual imperatives. Thus the Biblical Book of Proverbs gives expression to some eight hundred aphorisms of conduct, while it also teaches that virtue and goodness are wisdom and that wickedness and vice are folly. The righteous is wise, the wicked foolish. Wisdom is the moral conscience in action. One who finds this moral wisdom finds life. To hate evil is reverence for God, and reverence for God is the beginning of knowledge and of true wisdom (Psalm 111:10; Proverbs 1:7, 8:13, 9:10; Job 28:28; Ecclesiastes 12:13). In this spirit of sage moralizing the Book of Proverbs offers epitomized practical answers to the searcher after ethical wisdom.

However, the Jew has not closed his eyes to more speculative problems of life. These are searchingly and frankly explored in two other Biblical books, Job and Ecclesiastes. The Book of Job is perhaps the profoundest work ever written by man. It tells its symbolic story with deep reverence conjoined with unflinching probing. With sublime bravery of thinking it searchingly grapples with such questions as what is the meaning of human suffering? What is the answer to the problem of pain? Why does it often happen that trials come so undeservedly to the good and the pious? Job clung to his faith for the final answer, "I know that my Redeemer liveth" (19:25). Similarly the author of the Book of Eccle-

siastes gropes for light on the path through life. He sees with
vivid clarity such "vanities" as sensuality, self-indulgence,
amassing wealth that can never be used, miserliness, bitter
rivalries, anger, misgovernment, oppression, unremitting toil,
and unctuous righteousness. But he find life when wisely
lived to be eminently good and to be enjoyed by man. Neither
Job nor Ecclesiastes gives an absolute answer to all the
problems of life, for there are some questions that mortal
man cannot answer. But neither book yields to despairing
pessimism. The declaration, "vanity of vanities, all is vanity"
(Ecclesiastes 1:2) is not upheld by Ecclesiastes, yet neither
does he find the answer in an unreasoning, unquestioning
optimism. "The final word after all has been heard is revere
God *and* keep His commandments" (Ecclesiastes 12:13). Man
will find meaning and supreme purpose in life in a thinking
religious faith united with right conduct.

It was to preserve and transmit to mankind all these
teachings of the ancient Bible that the Jew has continued
to live. His work is not yet finished. To complete this mission
God has called on him to survive. "For as the new heaven
and the new earth which I will make shall remain before Me,
saith the Lord, so shall your seed and your name remain"
(Isaiah 66:22).

FOUR

THE NEXT TWO THOUSAND YEARS

MANY HAVE the impression that the message of Judaism stopped some nineteen centuries ago, or even earlier with the closing of the Hebrew Bible. The Jew rejoices in his Judaism because it is still, as it has always been, a living, developing religion which offers the way for happiness, for self-fulfilment in the present and for an unlimited vision of promise for the future. Its story did not come to an end with the completion of the Bible, nor did the history of the Jewish people close with the destruction of Jerusalem and their first commonwealth over twenty-five centuries ago.

Six and a half centuries after that, the all-powerful Roman Empire devastated the Jewish state, the Jewish people, their Temple and their Holy City. Some sixty years later, a last desperate revolt led by Bar Kochba against the overpowering Roman domination succeeded for a time in wresting Jerusalem from Roman hands, but after two and a half years of incredibly heroic struggle against overwhelming odds, in the year 135 crushing defeat came at Bethar upon the insurgent Jews. Then Jerusalem, the Holy City, was wiped from the map and given the name Aelia Capitolina. Jews were forbidden to enter it under pain of death, and public observance of the Sabbath and every other Jewish religious rite was sternly prohibited by the Roman conquerors. Some half a million Jews had perished in the struggle. But even this did not bring to a close the story of the Jew and his religion.

In the face of apparently total destruction of the organized Jewish people and the outlawing of their religion, how have they achieved the miracle of survival? To answer this question let us for a moment turn back to the end of Bible days. Half a century after the exiling of the Jews to Babylon two and a half millennia ago, numbers of them returned to their Promised Land. The last of the prophets, Haggai, Zechariah, and Malachi, spurred those who went back to rebuild their community as the People of the Book. Twelve centuries after Moses had created the Jewish nation by rescuing them from enslavement to a tyrannical ruler, the Maccabees had to recreate the Jewish people and their state. They established the principle of religious freedom and the right of men to national and cultural self-determination. In his subsequent world dispersion the Jew tended and carried with him the perpetual light of a living Judaism. Indeed, the rabbis say that wheresoever the Jewish people went the Divine Presence went with them. The Biblical verse I Samuel 2:27 has been translated as meaning that God had exiled Himself with them when they were slaves to Pharaoh in Egypt, also a verse in Isaiah (43:14) as showing that He had been with them in their exile in Babylon, and words in Deuteronomy (30:3) as promising that He will return with them from any future exile. It was the fact that in all his dispersion over the face of the globe the Jew tended the light of his faith which made it live on as a light for the world.

In the last centuries before the Christian era the Jewish diaspora had spread to Babylon, Persia, Egypt, Italy, and other lands bordering the Mediterranean Sea. After the

Roman scattering of the Jewish people, Jewish communities grew in numbers all over the Roman Empire. As time went on Jews found their way to all parts of Europe, to North Africa and the mountains of Abyssinia, to India and Cochin, to China, and to the remotest corners of the earth. In more recent centuries Jews were to be found among the pioneers in darkest Africa, among the earliest settlers in the western hemisphere, and among the founders of modern Australia. The world over they took their place with those opening up new lands for settlement. Everywhere they preserved their own religious tradition. Already in the days of their captivity in Babylonia in the sixth century before the common era the prophet Jeremiah (29:4–7) had sent God's word to the exiles, "Build houses and dwell in them and plant gardens and eat their fruit. Take wives and beget sons and daughters, and take wives for your sons and give your daughters to husbands, that they may bear sons and daughters and increase there and be not diminished. And seek the welfare of the city whither I have exiled you, and pray to the Lord for it, for in its welfare shall be your welfare." In the early part of the third century of the common era Mar Samuel laid it down as a principle governing life everywhere in the dispersion that the law of the land has binding power. The Bible with its Torah was the Jew's religious guide. Wherever the "tribe of the wandering feet" settled in any numbers, they would organize religious services and soon thereafter establish synagogues, the nucleating centers of Judaism. It was within the synagogue that the Biblical tradition of the fathers was preserved and, what is not so generally recognized, also progressively, developed in written and oral tradition.

Both have been fundamental. Two thousand years ago, it is told, a would-be proselyte to Judaism came to the rabbi Hillel and said that he was ready to accept the written law of Moses but not the oral tradition taught by the rabbis. Hillel replied that he was willing to receive him, and he began by teaching him the first two letters of the alphabet, aleph and beth. The next day at the second lesson he taught him the letter aleph as beth and beth as aleph. "No," said the man, "yesterday you taught me the other way round." Hillel's reply was, "You see? If you wish to accept even the most elementary facts in the written Torah you cannot commence to do this without also accepting the interpretation given to them by accepted spoken tradition. Without that you cannot begin to learn to read them, much less understand them."

The frontiers of Judaism have never been set with finality, even by the Bible itself. Even less has Judaism become a static tradition within the last two thousand years. The place of the Karaites in Jewish history strikingly exemplifies this. This little known group was a sect of fundamentalists that grew up in the early Middle Ages. With extreme rigidity they endeavored to limit their Judaism to their own strict and inflexible interpretation of the Bible. Their confining principles condemned the Karaites to petrification. They were repudiated by the main stream of creative Jewry, and they remained a small undeveloping group, and today they are all but extinct.

Judaism though essentially the product of Biblical days and of the Holy Land is a way of life that has been enriched in every generation and in many lands. The process began in the time of the Bible itself. The prophets and even the priests met ever-changing conditions by a continued developing organic detailed interpretation of the basic Torah. Indeed, in the very days of Moses there arose the need for interpreting the fundamental law in its application to new situations.

To give but one example. The sixth commandment decrees, "You shall not murder," or, as it is often put in the English

translation, "You shall not kill." That command would seem
at first sight transparently clear, simple and unexceptionable.
Yet how quickly it calls for interpretation in everyday life!
Does the command prohibit the taking of human life only
or does it apply equally to all living? May we kill animals?
May we kill them for food? May we kill noxious and danger-
ous beasts? May we kill to get fur or feathers or oil? Is killing
in sport, as in hunting, permissible? May we kill in scientific
research in the quest of healing or in the pursuit of knowledge? The obvious prohibition against taking of human life
arouses yet more baffling questions. May one kill in self-
defence? May one consent to fight in times of war? Is capital
punishment for crime permitted? Is euthanasia defensible?
When the lives of a mother and her child are threatened in
childbirth, may one of them be sacrificed to the other?

These questions could readily be multiplied, and they arise
with every generalized regulation. For example: "remember
the Sabbath day to keep it holy." This command has been
the subject of perennial discussion, interpretation, and religious regulation in every generation since the wandering
of the children of Israel in the desert of Sinai when a man was
found gathering sticks on the Sabbath day. The question was
then raised by the people as to whether what he was doing
constituted a violation of the law prohibiting work on the
Sabbath. The man was brought to Moses and Aaron and before all the congregation the inquiry took place as to what the
ruling should be (Numbers 15:32–36). Later the Torah
declares that "If there come up a matter too hard for you
in judgment . . . then you shall arise and go up to the place
which the Lord your God shall choose, and you shall come
to the priests, the Levites, and to the judge who shall be in
those days and you shall consult them, and they shall declare
to you the decision . . . And you shall observe to do according to all that they shall teach you" (Deuteronomy 17:8–10).

Two thousand and more years ago the rabbis continuing this corollary tradition of interpretation built it up in a progressively organized and authoritative way to meet ever changing conditions. The process of adjustment became the more imperatively called for after the Roman legions had ravaged the Jewish homeland and destroyed Jerusalem with its unitary and centralizing Temple. Fundamental was the "Torah Moses commanded us, an inheritance of the congregation of Jacob" (Deuteronomy 33:4). Of this Torah it is said, "Moses received the Torah from Sinai and transmitted it to Joshua. Joshua transmitted it to the elders; they handed it on to the prophets, and the prophets transmitted it to the men of the Great Assembly," who in turn handed it on to the rabbis. It was they who carried on the role of creative interpretation of the law, preventing its becoming fixed and finalized. Their reverent and unswerving devotion to the Biblical word was unquestioned. But they had the courage in the light of their understanding to explain its meaning in relation to changing conditions. They enriched and amplified the message of the Bible by interpreting and applying it to new circumstances.

In secular law a national constitution is necessarily the subject of continuing interpretive development. Though newly-formulated laws are ever evolving to meet new conditions, these must remain constitutional. In this spirit the constitution of the Torah has been continuously developed by the rabbis. There is a saying that every decision of an authoritative rabbi was already spoken at Mount Sinai. This is a daring figurative way of expressing the principle that all such flexible interpretation of the original constitution has the full authority of law. Life recognizes no standstill. The rabbis held that if you do not increase, you will decrease. They saw clearly that though a great past gave to the Jew his character, his inspiration, and his *raison d'être*, the past must not be allowed to become an inflexible bed of Procrustes.

This process of organic growth through constant illuminative interpretation is the contribution of the Pharisaic tradition to Judaism. A vast body of derived oral law grew up complementing the sacred writ. In all this there was no capricious change nor were there any abolitions prompted only by convenience. If in the religious celebration of the autumn harvest the Biblical word called for the use of a palm branch, branches of willow and myrtle, and a citron, these symbols were not explained away as inconvenient or outlived when virtually all the exiled Jewish people were no longer living as agriculturists on their own fields. If the Biblical word called for the New Year's summons being sounded on a ram's horn, the rabbis never for a moment considered that city-dwelling Jews could substitute for it a cornet or trumpet. They carried on unchanged the basic Biblical tradition that glowed ever more brightly as it accumulated the values of centuries of religious emotion and nostalgic associations.

Laws which in the Torah are expressed as succinct generalizations are necessarily interpreted and elaborated by the rabbis. Sometimes we cannot begin to understand the Biblical law without knowing its authoritative interpretation. One of the most generally misunderstood passages in the Bible is the law of damages. "Wound for wound, eye for eye, tooth for tooth, as he has caused a blemish in man so shall it be done to him" (Leviticus 24:20). This so-called *lex talionis* is in fact a principle of compensation, not of vengeance. The rabbis emphasize that it does not call for equal wounding of an assailant, but for damages actually equivalent to the hurts suffered by the victim. What underlies this law is calculated to mitigate and set a limit to conflicts and feuds, and restrain the impulse to harsh revenge. Except in the case of murder, it is value which has to be established for an eye, a tooth, etc. Is the hand of a young artist or musician of the same value as the hand of an old man? In the Middle Ages Jehudah Halevi commented that the law "embodies ideas antagonistic to common sense if interpreted literally . . . One person may die from a wound, whilst another may recover from the same." In practise this regulation has meant the payment of a just and equitable compensation for all. Nowhere do we find a decision such as in the case which came before the Greek legislator Solon when a man had knocked out the eye of a one-eyed man, and the order was given to have both eyes of the aggressor gouged out so that he also would be blinded. The Biblical law is also marked by a completely egalitarian outlook. In ancient days the penalty was likely to be lighter for members of the privileged classes. In Roman law the alien was almost without rights over against the citizen. Such discriminatory injustice in old-time German law is given expression in the opera Lohengrin: "The free man shall atone by the loss of his hand, the slave by the loss of his head." The Bible insists "You shall have one law for the stranger and for the native born" (Leviticus 24:22).

The earliest traditional detailed interpretations of the basic law of the Torah that were handed down from Bible times were put in writing early in the third century in a work called the Mishnah, "Repetition." This digest classifies Jewish law in six general divisions, a) agricultural, b) calendar, c) marriage, divorce, the home, d) civil and criminal law, e) Temple ritual, f) ritual purity. These six sections are further classified in sixty-three subdivisions. For its authority this code quotes the opinions and the decisions of scores of rabbis. It should be clearly understood that the rabbis were in no sense priests. They wore no ecclesiastical robes nor were they bound by any special regime of their own. The rabbi was a layman. In the time that he did not devote to learning he earned his living by working as a wood chopper, builder, tanner, blacksmith, scribe, shoemaker, tradesman, watchman, baker, charcoal burner, farmer, and so on.

The writing down of the Mishnah code did not spell finality to the development of Jewish law any more than had the written Biblical law on which it was based. Three hundred years later, around the year 500, there was compiled the Talmud, "Study," in which were set down extensions of the primary Biblical code to cover so far as possible every aspect of life. In the diffuse encyclopedic Talmud we find not only Biblical law but also botany, astronomy, medicine, hygiene, folklore, sociology, forms and ceremonies, human relations, and the most varied matters discussed in their widest range. Thus in the subject of class relations the Talmud amplifies the Biblical demand for the equal and undeviating justice that must be exercised on all classes of society. It demands that the employer should not eat fine bread while the employee eats coarse bread. The employer may not sleep on comfortable cushions while the employee sleeps on straw or hard boards. Employer and employee alike must have a standard of living that gives at least minimum decencies to both of them. The Bible calls for wages to be paid at nightfall when the day's work is done; the Shulhan Arukh, the later code of Jewish law based primarily on the Talmud, declared that anyone who withholds the fair wages of his employee is as though he took the employee's life itself.

There has been no hiatus in the continuity of the development of the Jewish code from Bible to Mishnah, from Mishnah to Talmud, and from the Talmud onward to our own day. This extensive growth continued through decisions of learned rabbis everywhere, through special collections of rulings, and through local customs and precedents. From the sixth century on it was influenced most notably by the standards set up by great rabbinical colleges in Babylonia. There Jews had for centuries been living in places such as Sura, Nehardea and Pumbeditha as organized communities in comparative freedom beyond the reach of the harshly dominating power of Rome. Decisions were made by the Geonim, "illustrious," rabbis who headed great academies and who furthered the lore of the Talmud compiled by their predecessors in Babylonia. Their only authority stemmed from their loving attachment to the Torah, their profound learning, their ethical conscientiousness, and their sensitive approach to human problems. Geographic, linguistic and cultural differences were overcome by these mighty spirits. Without their binding strength the diaspora might have hopelessly separated Jewry into fragments disconnectedly scattered over the lands between the Atlantic Ocean and Babylonia. It was the religious rulings of the rabbis in their all-embracing scope which bound and held the Jewish people together.

Over the centuries the literature which treats of every aspect of Jewish law and ritual became vast, diffused and discursive. The necessity of orderly compilation became imperative. Several incomplete summaries appeared in attempted codification of this unwieldy material. Following the tenth century, several efforts were made to put into writing an authoritative interpretation of Jewish tradition. It was the genius of Moses Maimonides (1135–1204) which gave birth to the first truly comprehensive and ordered code of Jewish law and lore. He designed his work which he called Hayad Hahazakah, "The Strong Hand," to be "a compendium of all the oral law, ordinances, customs, and decrees from the days of Moses our master to the close of the Talmud, including the interpretations of the Geonim since that time." This code of Maimonides served as the basis for all subsequent ones.

It was the Shulhan Arukh, "The Set Table," compiled by

Joseph Caro in the middle of the sixteenth century and greatly enriched by Moses Isserles (1510–1572) that became the authoritative digest of Jewish living which the age of printing helped make readily available everywhere. The Shulhan Arukh is divided into four main sections. The first and most popular section Orah Hayyim, "The Way of Life," deals with ritual and prayer, and the laws and practises of daily life, of the Sabbath, festivals and holy days. The second section, Yoreh Deah, "Teaching Knowledge," is of much more varied content. It includes the dietary laws and the laws and customs governing the prohibition of idolatry, the taking of interest, superstition, bodily uncleanliness and purification, vows and oaths, the honor due to parents, education, charity, circumcision, servants, proselytes, the scroll of the law, the mezuzah scroll on the door-post, forbidden mixtures, redemption of the first-born, separation of the dough, excommunication, visiting the sick, and mourning and burial. The third section, Eben Haezer, "The Stone of Help," summarizes the laws of marriage, divorce and the family; while the fourth division, Hoshen Mishpat, "The Breastplate of Justice," is a manual of Jewish civil law.

Let it not be thought that this virtually all-inclusive code sounded the finale to the symphony of living Judaism harmonized to a changing world. The Shulhan Arukh, this standard digest, has in its turn been subjected to innumerable glosses and commentaries in the progressive adjustment of Judaism to life. Authoritative Judaism has avoided paralyzing fundamentalism, static Karaism, and runaway variants.

The spirit of these thousands of regulations is strikingly expressed in the opening of the Shulhan Arukh. Joseph Caro begins the first chapter detailing the first duty on awakening in the morning with the words, "One should show himself strong as a lion on arising in the morning for the service of his Creator." To this Moses Isserles adds, drawing on Maimonides, " 'I keep the Lord before me at all times' (Psalm 16:8) is a great principle in the Torah and in the qualities of the righteous who walk before God. For a man's settled character, his movements, and his activities when he is alone in his own home are not the same as they would be were he in the presence of a great king. Nor is his converse with his family or friends as it would in the presence of a king. Therefore how much the more conscientious will a man be when he takes to heart the fact that the king before whom he stands is the great King, the Holy One, blessed be He, whose glory fills the whole world, and that it is He who stands over man and sees all that he does, as it is written, 'Can a man hide in secret places and I would not see him, saith the Lord' (Jeremiah 23:24). When he realizes that, there will immediately come to him the spirit of reverence and awe before God and humility before Him at all times, and he will feel no mortifying abasement when men sneer at him for his service of God."

In view of much current misunderstanding, it cannot be emphasized often enough that being a Jew has not meant being cramped by legalism though Judaism is based on the laws laid down in the Torah which have been developed from Bible days, and progressively written down in the Mishnah, the Talmud, the Code of Maimonides, the Shulhan Arukh, and an unbroken flood of commentaries. The rabbis have always insisted on *kavvanah*, a Hebrew term which means devoted attention and intention in the carrying out of ritual and in the utterance of prayer. There is, of course, the possibility that regimentation in religious life may degenerate into formalism and externalism. But spiritual alertness has prevented the letter of the Jewish law from dominating or injuring its spirit.

The Hebrew name for Jewish law is *halakhah*, "the way to go." The law's formulated rulings were illumined by the creativity of the rabbis in their *haggadah*, "recital." This was a literary stream of illuminating writing which abounds in stories, sermons, anecdotes, fables, sagas, poetry, parables, allegories, wise sayings, emotional appeals, and spiritual effusions of many kinds. It expressed the popular soul and met the popular need. Literacy has been common among Jews, especially with men, even in the dark ages when generally only the clergy could read and write. Though not every man in a Jewish community was a skilled student of the law, yet all, children and adults, women and men alike, would be apt to know moral apothegms such as those which the Mishnah legal code collects in its tractate Pirke Aboth. These chapters of sayings of the fathers are popularly studied on certain Sabbaths in the year, and because of their richly stimulating content and their association with the poetic atmosphere of the Sabbath they hold a warm place in the heart.

Haggadah and halakhah have always complemented one another. There is no disparity or opposition between the normative rulings of the halakhah and the imaginative flights of fancy and outpourings of the haggadah. Maimonides, the outstanding codifier of Biblical and Talmudic law, was also the author of the moral and spiritual masterpiece, "The Guide of the Perplexed." Abraham ibn Ezra (1092–1167), a keen commentator on the Biblical text, was also a writer of intensely devotional hymns. Joseph Caro, the compiler of the Shulhan Arukh's code of laws, had the soul of a supreme mystic. Judaism's all-penetrating concern with every implication of the Torah's laws has not fostered dry formal scholasticism. Its ritual is an expression of a religious discipline which endeavors to seek out the utmost implications of the divine commands.

The rabbis point out that no two prophets in the Bible give their message in the same style. An Ezekiel speaks like a villager, an Isaiah like one at home in the royal court. The rabbis themselves frequently varied from one another in their rulings; yet their differences did not break the unifying conformity of religious observance. Long continued influences of environment and geography are reflected in minor deviations in customs, some of which have developed striking character and most of which have assumed the strength of sanctions. Inevitably there developed many differences in local custom, but not in basic Jewish law. Its teachings have remained the central influence which has held Jews together however widely they may have been scattered, and whatever differences of local color might have developed.

Over the centuries three main groupings have come to be recognized: Ashkenazi, Sephardi, and Oriental. The most numerous are the Ashkenazim, the Hebrew word for German. Their historic background is Northern, Central and Eastern European. Their pronunciation of Hebrew varies from the Sephardi and Oriental, and the colloquial language of many of them since medieval times has been a form of Middle High German known as Yiddish. The Sephardim, Jews with a Spanish background—the word Sepharad in Hebrew is Spain—scattered from the Iberian Peninsula after their expulsion from Spain in 1492 to the broad reaches of the Mediterranean basin, to Northern and Western Europe and to the New World. The colloquial tongue of many of them was based on old Spanish and their Hebrew pronunciation has been adopted as standard in today's revived land of Israel. Oriental Jews who have lived in the Middle East for two thousand years are close to the Sephardim in their traditions of language and ritual and are often grouped together with them because of these and other similarities.

Minor differences in custom mark these groups. The rabbis accepted these variants, even when, as occasionally happened, they touched on the interpretation of Jewish law. No rabbi, however great and eminent, could speak with authoritarian finality, nor could he canonize his own views. He could not preclude other rabbis from using equal freedom of judgment. The masterly code drawn up by Moses Maimonides, decisive though it was in general, was not spared keenly critical examination by other scholars. The subsequent code, the Shulhan Arukh, was quickly extended by the inclusion of thousands of practises customary in lands which Joseph Caro, its compiler, did not know.

Beyond any range of difference in outlook or custom the conservation of basic traditions is crucial for the Jew. During two thousand years of a wandering that was all too often impelled by relentless persecution, his very existence as a Jew has been made possible by his loyalty to his heritage and its ineffable significance for him. It is this which has preserved him. Today and tomorrow it must preserve him and with him the message he carries.

FIVE

THE HOLY LAND

A N ESSENTIAL formative element in the Jewish psyche, which neither anthropology nor geography can explain, is the grip of the Land of Israel, the Holy Land. The land of the Bible has been of the bedrock in Judaism and in the history of the Jewish people for four thousand years. Ordinarily, transplanted individuals and their immediate descendants preserve a sentimental attachment to their land of origin. One, two, or perhaps three generations may continue to speak, or at least understand, its language and sing its songs. Beyond that only a faint memory of the old family background is likely to live on. Nineteen hundred years ago the Roman legions destroyed the Jewish state; but through all these centuries of dispersion of the Jewish people from their historic homeland, Zion has dwelt in their consciousness as a spiritual anchorage with unbroken vitality and unfading vividness.

The Hebrew Bible is in every sense a book of the Promised Land, which it made into the Holy Land. When the background of its story is Mesopotamia, as in the early narrative about Abraham, or Egypt, as in the record of Pharaoh's enslavement of the children of Israel, even in those narratives it is the Holy Land to which the eyes are lifted as the focal land of promise and fulfilment.

The whole of Judaism is redolent of that land. Its religious calendar is determined by it. All festivals except Purim are associated with its harvest celebrations. The festival of Tabernacles recreates the harvest booth of the forefathers in that land, and around the synagogue the Holy Land's palm branch and citron are borne in the procession of the Hosannas. In welcoming the Sabbath or a festival or any other joyous religious occasion, the Jew chants a blessing over a cup of sacramental wine in a tradition harking back to the Land of Israel and its vineyards. At the most meteorologically varied points on earth, be it Stockholm or Capetown, Calcutta or Buenos Aires, the Jew prays on the Passover that dew may be plentiful during the coming rainless summer in the land of the Bible. At Tabernacles, without regard to his own local geography, he prays that that land may not lack rain in the coming months. On the fast of Ab he chants dirges and Jeremiah's Book of Lamentations to recall the disasters wrought on Jerusalem by its enemies. The New Year for Trees is celebrated all over the world as the day when the sap rises and spring arrives in the Promised Land. The two-day observance of festivals originated in countries neighboring upon the Holy Land in an attempt to synchronize with the observances in Jerusalem.

Synagogue architecture is oriented toward Jerusalem. When standing in prayer, whether in synagogue, in the home or anywhere he may be, the worshiper turns in the direction of the site of the Temple of old in Zion. The prayers intoned in the historic language of the Holy Land, the Hebrew of its Bible, keep Zion vividly alive in the consciousness. Recurrently they answer the Psalmist's call (122:6) "Pray for the peace of Jerusalem," and express the hope of Zion rebuilt and redeemed. For generations it was a custom that is still occasionally seen, to leave as a sobering reminder of the destruction of Jerusalem an unfinished square on the living room wall facing toward the Holy City. The familiar breaking of a glass at the conclusion of the traditional wedding ceremony is symbolic of Jerusalem's shattered state, and recalls the Psalmist's cry (137:5, 6) "If I forget thee, O Jerusalem, may my right hand fail. May my tongue cleave to the roof of my mouth if I remember thee not, if I do not set Jerusalem above my chiefest joy."

As a prelude to the traditional blessings after a meal on Sabbaths and festivals the family at the table sings the one hundred and twenty-sixth Psalm, recalling that "when the Lord restored those who returned to Zion we were as in a dream. Then was our mouth filled with laughter and our tongue with joyous song." In such ways the memory of Zion is ever with the Jew throughout his life. When death comes, earth from the Holy Land is set in the coffin, symbolically uniting him with the sacred soil.

Zion has been the Holy Land's spiritual center since the time of King David. The world knows not a few Holy Cities such as Lhasa in Tibet, or Benares in India. Jerusalem is holy for three of the world's great faiths. The Moslem calls it El Kuds, a shortening of the designation Beit el Kuds, i.e., the home of the sacred shrine in Arabic. Yet for the Moslems, Mecca is the holy city par excellence, and exclusively theirs, so much so that those of faiths other than Islam are prohibited from entering it. Jerusalem with its associations with the life of Jesus and the disciples has always been a Holy City for the Christian world. In the Middle Ages many were the wars of the Crusades that were waged in the effort to bring it under Christian rule. Yet millions of Christians call Rome the Holy City. For the Jew only Jerusalem is the Holy City.

Its uniqueness as the pivotal holy shrine is a recurrent and burning theme of the Biblical prophets. After its destruction by the Babylonians, prayers for its rebuilding and for the return to it stand out in heart-piercing utterances of prophets and Psalmist. In rhapsodic vision, the Holy City of the Jews is seen as eventually the teacher for all humanity. "From Zion shall go forth divine teaching and the word of the Lord from Jerusalem" (Isaiah 2:3, Micah 4:2). It has been overshadowed materially many times in many ways, whether by "the great city" of Nineveh, by Tyre with its world commerce, by Rome with its empire-building legions, and by many a capital city in the modern world. Yet little Jerusalem remains the Holy City not only for Jews but for a mighty segment of mankind.

Twenty-five hundred years ago, following the permission and encouragement given by Cyrus, ruler of the Persian empire, many Jews after some seventy years of exile returned from Babylon to their ancestral land. Those who remained in Babylon were urged to help their brethren who were going back to rebuild the homeland and Zion. In all subsequent centuries, synagogues and Jewish communities far and wide have regarded it as a sacred obligation to collect funds to aid Jewish settlement in the Holy Land. Whatever might have been the hardships, intrepid individual Jewish pilgrims in ever growing numbers made a reality of their prayers and hopes by returning to the Promised Land. Jehudah Halevi the brilliant twelfth-century Spanish Jewish poet, gave up his life of comfort to settle in the land of which he had so often sung. In his ode to Zion he wrote as translated by Alice Lucas:

> Oh, who will lead me on
>   To seek the spots where in far distant years
> The angels in their glory dawned upon
>   Thy messengers and seers?

Oh, who will give me wings
  That I may fly away,
And there at rest from all my wandering,
  The ruins of my heart among thy ruins lay?

I'll bend my face unto thy soil, and hold
  Thy stones as precious gold.
And when in Hebron I have stood beside
  My fathers' tombs, then will I pass in turn
Thy plains and forest wide,
  Until I stand on Gilead and discern
Mount Hor and Mount Abarim 'neath whose crest
  Thy luminaries twain, thy guides and beacons rest.

The Lord desires thee for His dwelling place
  Eternally, and bless'd
Is he whom God has chosen for the grace
  Within thy courts to rest.
Happy is he that watches, drawing near,
  Until he sees thy glorious lights arise,
And over whom thy dawn breaks full and clear
  Set in the orient skies.
But happiest he who with exultant eyes
  The bliss of thy redeemed ones shall behold,
And see thy youth renewed as in days of old.

SIX

OPTIMISM AND FAITH

A MYRIAD of influences from the past have determined
the evolution of Judaism and have created the Jew.
But though he be bound in the line of historic events, it is
not only backwards that he looks. In ancient Rome Horace
asserted that while the age of his parents was worse than
that of their forebears, in its turn it had produced his generation yet more worthless than they, while his own age was
destined to bring forth a progeny still more depraved. This
ultimate in pessimism in the evaluation of the course of
human history sharply contrasts with the Messianic optimism
of the Jew. He stands out among the peoples and the religions
of the earth in not setting the golden age in the past. He has
followed the counsel of the sage Ecclesiastes, who said (7:10),
"Say not how was it that the former days were better than
these, for not from wisdom do you put this question." The
Torah's unsparing divulgence of the faults of the children
of Israel in the days of Moses and in later Biblical days, and
the scathing denunciations by the prophets of the evils they
beheld have never allowed the Jew to create the defeatist
legend of perfection in the past.

Judaism looks to the future for the Golden Age, and that it is which we of the present have to struggle to build. Righteousness, justice, law, human brotherhood, peace, are not yearned-for memories from a mythological yesterday; they are ideals proclaimed from of old to be striven for today and realized tomorrow. The highest purpose of mankind in the present must be to help establish a future of Messianic blessing. The Jewish outlook on life does not comfort slaves with hope for reward in a future life, bidding them accept slavery because of ultimate recompense to be accorded beyond this earth. The call first voiced by Moses in Egypt bidding men be free is continuously sounded. Judaism does not tell men not to resist evil, an attitude which may pave the way for society's falling into the power of the unscrupulous. It summons everyone to combat evil and set up good on earth, not in a heavenly hereafter. A theme which runs through the Biblical laws is "You shall put away the evil from your midst" (Deuteronomy 13:6, 17:7, 21:21, 24:7). The medieval poet and philosopher Jehudah Halevi summed up this outlook when he said that "the prevalent custom among us is not to separate ourselves from the world nor to despise it . . . but to seek it." Judaism finds no compensation for evils on earth in the idea of transmigration, nor in the lure of a heavenly recompense for wretched and unfulfilled lives, nor in the anodyne of personal withdrawal into contemplative otherworldliness. Man is summoned to remake this world through action with the vision before his eyes of God and life's potential goodness.

Such a faith born of optimism engenders happiness. Being a Jew makes me happy. Judaism sees virtue in enjoying life and trying to improve it. This teaching stands out as the more precious and psychologically the more significant when one remembers how over the centuries the Jew has been forced to know so much sorrow and tragedy. Yet however menacing

and dark the world about him may have been, his faith in
the potential and the essential goodness of life never faded
or failed.

This optimism that sees good arising out of apparent evil
is graphically illustrated in a folk tale in the Talmud. It is
related of the famous Rabbi Akiba that traveling on his
mule he came one evening to a village. The inn was full and
he could be given no accommodation for the night. So he
retired to a quiet spot in the dark nearby woods. There
mishap after mishap occurred. His lamp was blown out by
the wind. A cock he was carrying with him was killed by a
weasel. His mule was killed by a lion. In the morning he
learned that shortly before dawn the village had been entered
by marauders and those in the inn had been injured or killed.
Had his lamp been alight, had his cock crowed or his mule
brayed, he might also have fallen into the hands of the bandits.
Truly, said Rabbi Akiba, all is for the best. In one's journey
throughout life one must see how good may arise from mis-
fortune. *Gam zo letovah*—"this too has good in it"—has
become one of the most popular of Jewish dicta.

Such optimism has been a powerful factor in preserving
the Jew in his difficult journey through the ages. He has
had to live under the shadow of oppression and persecution,
even unto our own days when he had to experience the
hideous Nazi infamy of concentration camps, gas chambers,
and the organized insensate sadistic annihilation of 6,000,000
Jews. All too often he has seen beneath the surface veneer
of our civilization men transformed into amoral monsters.
Yet despite the gloom into which he was thrust, he has
not given way to despair. With his triumphant optimism
which the encompassing realities so often made it difficult
to justify, he never lost heart to face life with hope. He
always looked, prayed and worked for a future that would
give comfort for the sorrows of the past. The prophets taught

him to regard suffering as a discipline for mankind's soul
and his eventual salvation. This world must not be thought
of as a vale of tears. Life can be made and must be made good.
It is not inherently evil and endangering to the soul. It is
intrinsically good and capable of ever greater betterment if
we but will it.

In the Jewish outlook on life Satan appears but rarely and
dimly. Only three times in the Bible (Job 1, 2; Zechariah
3:1, 2; I Chronicles 21:1) does the Adversary, for that is the
meaning of the Hebrew term "Satan," appear as a definite
figure. In each case he is represented allegorically as the
symbolic accuser of man. It is true that in post-Biblical days
the Satan-Accuser often came to be regarded as symbolizing
man's inclination to do evil; but he was hardly pictured as
the devil against whose demonic attempts to corrupt and
destroy the human soul man must struggle desperately
throughout life. The Jewish recognition of one sole God
has never been compromised by a duality created from the
impersonation of evil. The prayer book daily recalls the
words heard by Isaiah (45:7) as spoken by God, "I form the
light and create darkness, I make peace and create evil;
I am the Lord who does all these things." The world is not
swinging in physical space or in the human spirit between
a deity and a devil, between good and evil, between heaven
and hell. It is not the battleground between God and the
devil.

This permeating optimism extends from man's spirit to
his physical being. The opening chapters of the Bible sound
the keynote in stating majestically that man is created in
the image of God. The human body is a God-given blessing;
it is not sinful flesh. George Eliot rightly speaks of "Judaism's
reverence for the human body which lifts the needs of
normal life into religion."

The exercise of bodily functions is regarded by the Jew

as natural and good. He thanks and blesses God for such physical experiences as smelling the fragrance of flowers, hearing the clap of thunder, seeing lightning, the ocean or a beautiful landscape, washing the hands, and partaking of food and drink. The body does not endanger the soul, for both are good and derived from the one supreme source. Natural impulses such as the sex urge or hunger are goodly instruments which God implanted for man's advantage and development. Without them men would not feel impelled to build homes, marry and beget children. One rabbi says that the most highly praised element in the work of creation (Genesis 1:31), "And God saw all that He had made and behold it was *very* good," refers to man's natural impulses.

Jehudah Halevi in the twelfth century declared that "the divine law imposes no asceticism on us. It rather desires that we should keep the equipoise, and should grant every mental and physical faculty its due. . . . Your contrition on a fast day brings you no nearer to God than your joy on the Sabbath and the festival days that springs from a devout heart." Judaism sees no world-serving virtue in monastic seclusion and its social isolation, or in fleeing the world and renouncing its blessings. The Biblical law places only the leper and the unclean outside the camp. Of old, Ecclesiastes warned (7:16), "be not righteous overmuch . . . wherefore destroy yourself?" Later, Rabbi Simon complemented this by his tenet, "be not evil in your own sight." When on the Day of Atonement even the most pious and saintly associate themselves with the community in a repeated, lengthy, detailed confession of sins which have assuredly not all been committed by every individual, it is a superb hyperbole expressive of the sensitive moral responsibility of one for all and all for one. If anyone in the community has deceived, slandered, been dishonest, or has done any wrong, everyone shares his guilt.

This does not mean that at times, and with varying significance, Jewish spiritual thinkers did not experiment with aspects of religious experience tangential to the theology and philosophy of the main stream of Judaism. We learn from Josephus, the first century historian, and now also from the newly discovered Dead Sea Scrolls, about the Essenes of two thousand years ago. They followed the Biblical Nazirites and Rechabites in protesting against social corruptions by harking back to drastic simplicity of living. Like the Nazirites, who were individuals, and like the little coterie of the nomadic Rechabites, they remained a small group outside the main stream of Jewish life. Though their spirituality and mystic approach to God often reappeared in Jewish history, their monastic tendencies did not. The Essenes withdrew from the organized life of human society not because of a belief that life and the body are evil, but in an effort to escape those who had corrupted it and to find in prayer, contemplation and service the inexpressible goodness of communion with God. When in his self-imposed separatism the pious Nazirite found that he had been subjected to contamination, even involuntarily, the Bible enjoins that he bring a sin-offering. This, the rabbis said, was because he had renounced the joys of life symbolized by the wine which the Psalmist (104:15) says "rejoices the heart of man." This was also the conviction which they expressed when they dubbed as a sinner one who gives himself to frequent fasting. Nazirite asceticism, the hermit's seclusion and austerity, pillar saints, glorification of hardship, renunciation of the world's blessings, and other self-centered and self-created quests of personal salvation, may indeed come dangerously near to intensifying the very evils that they seek to overcome. They take potently righteous individuals out of the arena of active life. They divert powerful spiritual qualities from cooperating with organized social forces that battle evil. They set goals which the normal man repudiates and thus create moral confusion. Moses Maimonides, outstanding Jewish thinker of the Middle Ages, said, "Let one not say that because the desire for pleasures may lead on to evil I will abstain altogether from the joys of life and find safety in the extreme of total abstention." He considered it a negation of virtue and not righteous living and holiness to avoid marriage, refrain from eating meat, refuse to touch wine, abandon the comforts of a home, wear sackcloth, and in general subjugate and mortify the flesh. He declared that one who gives himself to such un-Jewish practises of renunciation and impoverishment of life is a sinner. Rab, one of the greatest rabbis of the Talmudic era, declared that on the day of judgment every one will have to give an accounting for every legitimate pleasure which he had not sought to enjoy. In emphasizing the happiness one should find in life the rabbis recalled the Biblical words (I Chronicles 16:27), "Strength and joy are in His place," giving divine sanction to a sound body and a happy spirit.

Judaism holds that when man is born he is not enchained by original sin. He is inherently good and dowered with a moral conscience that is reinforced by freedom of will. The great rabbi Akiba said that although everything is foreseen by God, yet He has given man free will. Maimonides, the medieval philosopher, stated that everyone altogether of his own free will may be as righteous as Moses or as sinful as Jeroboam, wise or foolish, kindly or cruel. Sin exists, and temptation is always with us. But by his own strength man can overcome them. At the very beginning of the Bible story Cain is told that "sin couches at the door, and unto you is its desire, but you may rule over it" (Genesis 3:7). Man is not doomed to will the good and yet do evil. With goodness innate in him he can and must be the architect of his own life. Freedom of moral will is cardinal in Judaism.

The Jew does not regard the world as a moral chaos that

should be fled, but as a society that can be fashioned in ever
upward progress despite the evil that lurks beneath the
surface of our civilization and threatens to destroy it. The
Jewish outlook fervently holds that man and life are inherently good. We may remind ourselves again that in the
Biblical story we are told that when each day God looked on
His work of creation He saw that it was good, but on the
sixth day after He made man He saw that it was very good
(Genesis 1:4, 10, 18, 21, 25, 31).

In a similar spirit of optimism Judaism evaluates the
reality and meaning of suffering. With Rabbi Yannai it
admits that we can explain neither the prosperous security
that often seems to come to the sinful nor the sufferings which
may afflict the virtuous. Ha-Adam, man, no longer lives in
the Elysian bliss of a Garden of Eden. Toil and hardship
began after he ate of the tree of knowledge. When knowledge,
thought, self-consciousness and moral choice entered human
experience, life could no longer be vegetative and untroubled.
Ecclesiastes summarily declared (1:18) that "he who increases
knowledge increases sorrow." Was he anticipating the conquest of the atom? And is not the lesson taught at the very
gates of Eden one that we need to learn today? Toil, trouble,
the agony of decision, the acceptance of suffering, these and
much more are the lot of man who has eaten of the tree of
knowledge and who must learn with heartache the power
that this gives him.

A disciplinary and challenging measure of hardship is one
of the conditions of life. It must be made to strengthen our
moral fibre and bring out the best that is in us. Judaism
consistently teaches that just as a baby must learn to walk
physically, so all of us, who in the last analysis are children,
must learn to walk through life psychologically, morally,
spiritually. Struggle, hardship, toil, difficulty—these are part
of the curriculum in the school of man's experience. If you

want life, the rabbis pithily said, you must also know suffering, and better is one thing obtained through effort, difficulty and trial than a hundred which come in ease. Some rabbis say we should bless God for the troubles that befall us no less than for the good. Sweet may be the uses of adversity. We do not hold that trial and suffering should shatter faith. In point of historic fact, the more cruelly the outside world made Jews suffer, the brighter seemed to burn the flame of faith within the synagogue and the home. The louder the shouts of the murderous mobs in the ghetto, the pale, or the concentration camp, the more intently the Jew listened for the footsteps of God's messenger on the mountain tops bearing the tidings of eventual redemption.

Judaism has ever clung to the vision of man's boundless potential for good. It has never abandoned the Psalmist's faith (8:6) that man can be little less than divine and crowned with glory and majesty. Because of this optimistic teaching of human potential I wish to remain a Jew. I rejoice that I am not led to seek bliss through a suppression of my normal personality on the one hand, and on the other through dependence on a life to be. Lulling the yearning of the heart does not satisfy the questioning mind. To maintain that the greater the sufferings and sorrows in this world the greater the reward and the bliss in the world to come may all too readily become an opiate reconciling to needless suffering. "Be not grieved, for the joy of the Lord is your strength" (Nehemiah 8:10), "a cheerful heart is a good medicine" (Proverbs 17:22), and "the light is sweet and a pleasant thing it is for the eyes to see the sunlight. So if a man live many years, let him rejoice in them all" (Ecclesiastes 11:7, 9).

SEVEN

MIND AND SPIRIT

EMETH, the Hebrew word for truth, is according to the rabbis, the seal of God. The three letters, which spell the word are Aleph, Mem, Tav, the first, the middle and the last letters of the Hebrew alphabet. The lesson is clear, say the rabbis, from beginning to end all must be truth and the quest of truth. Judaism does not conflict with reason. Unlike religions which are overwhelmingly speculative and transcendental, and unlike creedal religions which demand that belief override all mental questioning, Judaism allows and indeed calls for open-minded inquiry. Moses Mendelssohn (1729–1786) emphasized that its primary teachings not only can be understood by the human mind but they can also be attested by it. Six centuries earlier Moses Maimonides had said that one should never abandon reason. In Judaism there is no dualism of faith and reason in warring antinomy. The Bible asks for a thoughtful, not an unquestioning, faith. As we have seen, the Books of Job and Ecclesiastes included in the Bible as part of the faith of the Jew, establish man's right to apply brave inquiry to all the questionings that may come to his soul. The summons of the Bible is less a call to believe in dogmas than it is a command to know, understand, and act. Of old, Rabbi Eleazar ben Azaryah epigrammatically declared that where there is no knowledge there is no understanding, and where there is no understanding there is no knowledge. There were three reasons which made Einstein declare that he was thankful to be heir to the Jewish tradition. The first was its love of justice, and the second the desire for personal independence. The third was the pursuit of knowledge for its own sake. The great rabbinic scholar Elijah Gaon (1720–1797) said that were all the teachings of the Torah to be miraculously revealed to him it would not make him happy, because it is the effort of study which gives to knowledge its worth, and it is study of the Torah which brings out the value of its practise.

The very word Torah, it has been pointed out, means guidance, instruction, teaching. Three times a day in his basic prayer, the Amidah, the Jew prays for knowledge, understanding, and enlightenment. Each morning in the prayer leading up to his fundamental declaration of faith in the one God he asks that he may have a heart of understanding and discernment so that he may hearken to the teachings of the Torah and learn and transmit them. Rabbi Simeon, son of Rabban Gamliel, said that not learning but doing is the essential. Under the vindictive edicts of the Roman emperor Hadrian which made the public observance of many a Jewish ritual law subject to the severest punishments, even death, the rabbis in solemn secret conclave discussed whether the first essential was study of the Torah or religious ritual practise. Some not unexpectedly said that practise must be given preference. But Rabbi Akiba took the stand that study of the Torah is ultimately the more important. The final decision of the rabbis agreed with him, for ignorance can make practise a meaningless automatism, whereas study tends to encourage action and give ever deeper meaning to religious practise.

Knowledge is power. It has given man undreamed of mastery over the physical world. When soulless it begets brute force, techniques of war, and ability to wreak colossal evil. Therefore the passionate insistence of Judaism has been to bind knowledge with reverence for God, giving man power to do prodigious good by transforming his knowledge into wisdom.

Centuries ago Rabbi Eleazar ben Azaryah declared that where there is no wisdom there is no reverence, and where there is no reverence there is no wisdom. The Book of Proverbs (3:13–18) forthrightly proclaims that "happy is the man who finds wisdom and the man who gets understanding . . . all the things you can desire are not to be compared with it. Length of days is in its right hand, in its left hand are riches and honor. Its ways are ways of pleasantness, and all its paths are peace. It is a tree of life to those who lay hold on it, and happy is everyone who holds fast." Repeatedly the Bible asserts that "the beginning of wisdom is reverence for God" (Psalm 111:10; Proverbs 1:7, 9:10; Job 28:28; Ecclesiastes 12:13). In the Bible and in Judaism wisdom is a moral term. Mysticism and rationality in religion are reciprocals that should mutually control one another. As a religious faith Judaism has held itself clear of extravagant emotionalism through a balancing emphasis on the intellect expressing itself in study and learning. The literacy of the Jewish people made available not only to the rabbi but to every individual the study of the Bible and its derivative literature. Readings from the Bible are central in all important synagogue services. The prayer book itself contains many extracts from rabbinic writings. The Book of Proverbs declares that (8:35) "he who turns away his ear from hearing Torah, even his prayer is an abomination," while he who finds God through knowledge finds life.

However, there are limits to knowledge. Moses was dramatically taught that one cannot see God face to face (Exodus 33:18–23). The Talmud relates that the Roman Emperor Hadrian scorning the Jewish faith asked Rabbi Joshua ben Hananyah to show him God. The rabbi replied, "Look at the sun," to which the emperor replied, "That is impossible." "If, then," retorted the rabbi, "you cannot look upon one of God's servants, how can you hope to see God face to face?"

God is the infinite cosmic God. The desire to understand the mysteries of this universe which modern man associates with the scientific mind of the Keplers, the Newtons and the Einsteins of history, is an expression of man's faith in the rationality of the world. In the Bible, and especially in its Wisdom literature, we find eloquent examples of the inquiring mind. The frontiers of human perception were challengingly expressed in the Book of Job (11:7, 8): "Can you find out the deep things of God, can you attain to the purposes of the Almighty? High as heaven, what can you do? Deeper than the nether world, what can you know?" The Bible is not a textbook of cosmology, geology, biology, or any other science. Yet in setting up religious regulations for living it draws on many confirmed scientific facts. Thus the Torah goes into precise detail about such matters as eugenic marriage controls, the institution of quarantine, and the treatment of skin diseases. The rabbinic development of the Biblical code continued the synthesis of science and religion. It probed deeply into anatomy in formulating the laws governing food. It drew on botany and agronomy in its agricultural legislation. It explored physiology and medicine in laying down laws of health. It necessarily delved deeply in astronomy and mathematics in determining the Jewish calendar. All this conscientious work in the field of science was done in the name of religion. Rabbi Eleazar Hisma roundly declared that astronomical and mathematical computations are incidental to religious learning. In the Talmud it is said that one who has the opportunity of studying astronomy and who does not take advantage of it is sinning by shutting his eyes to a recognition of God's creative work in the universe. It is a religious duty frankly and freely to search for truth, the seal of God.

Maimonides who lived in the dark era of the Middle Ages frankly declared that one who wishes to attain human perfection must in the first place study logic. Then one must study mathematics, then physics, and finally metaphysics. In this way, he held, one will come to his religion through all the tests of reason. Similarly Bahya ibn Pakuda in the eleventh century summed up this point of view in the following words: "The noblest of the gifts which God bestowed on His human creatures . . . is Wisdom. This constitutes the life of their spirit . . . Wisdom falls into three divisions. The first division is the science of created things . . . This deals with the essential and accidental properties of material bodies. The second division consists of the ancillary sciences, such as arithmetic, geometry, astronomy, or music. The third department . . . treats of the knowledge of God, blessed be He, and of the knowledge of His law and so forth. All the sciences are gates which the Creator has opened to rational beings through which they may attain to a comprehension of religion and of the world."

By itself science as we use the term today does not give a complete picture of reality. It is concerned with describing material processes and physical facts rather than with their potential meaning and value in human life. It may usefully focus attention on man's bodily kinship with the ape, or it may present man in geological time as a speck of dust momentarily flashing in the sunshine. The ever-growing value of science when applied in technology can by itself neither assure human progress nor give to life meaning and purpose. Invaluable as is psychology, it has little to say about man's spiritual aspirations. Science cannot comfort in sorrow, or feelingly interpret the good, the beautiful, joy, sorrow, love, and faith. Einstein affirmed that science without religion is lame, religion without science is blind. Science by itself can teach man to fly and can wipe out diseases; but science by itself without the complement of religion can also wipe out man with poison gas and atomic bombs. The very opening chapter of the Bible sets man into perspective in the universe of science. He figures as the climax of physical creation.

"When I behold Thy heavens, the work of Thy fingers, the moon and the stars which Thou hast established, what is frail man that Thou art mindful of him, the son of man that Thou takest thought of him? Yet Thou hast made him but little less than divine, and dost crown him with glory and majesty" (Psalm 8:4 6).

In Judaism science and religion are in harmonious synthesis as complementary aspects of the quest of truth in a unitary concept of life. Corollary to the oneness of God is the unity of the universe, the human mind, and the forces that move man's spirit. Every aspect of life, and science is but one of them, makes its contribution to the whole, of which the moving spirit is the one God. The totality of existence is a unity full of significance. The farthest vision of science cannot see beyond God. The Psalmist realized this when he exclaimed (139:7–10), "Whither can I go from Thy spirit? Or whither can I flee from Thy presence? If I ascend unto heaven, Thou art there. Or if I make the netherworld my bed, lo, Thou art there. Were I to take wings with the morning's light or dwell in the uttermost parts of the west, also there Thy hand would lead me, Thy right hand would

hold me." A scoffing questioner came to Rabbi Meir and
asked him how it was possible for this God who fills heaven
and earth to have revealed Himself to Moses within the
narrow confines of the tabernacle. In reply Rabbi Meir took
two mirrors, one large and one small, and showed his questioner how he could be seen in both of them. He is the God
who "dwells in the high and holy place, and also with him
who is of contrite and humble spirit" (Isaiah 57:15).

A world of science alone would indeed be bleak. Life
if appraised by reason alone would be coldly colorless. If
one were to look on life only through rationalistic eyes, he
would hardly be responsive to such transcendent spiritual
calls as that of love. With all its rationalistic realism and
insistence on thinking and free inquiry, Judaism has never
sunk into scholasticism. It is organically and inseparably
permeated with faith and emotion.

This emotion sometimes soars into the transcendentalism
of Cabbalistic rapture and ecstasy. The mysticism of the
Cabbalah, "tradition lore," came to high expression in
Safed in the Holy Land in the sixteenth century. Its most
popular outpouring came in the eighteenth century in Eastern
Europe as a result of the influence of the sensitively devout
soul of Israel Baal Shem Tov. He brought the joyous light
and glamor of mystic faith to many of the humble and poor
masses. He said that if not everyone could be learned, everyone could be pious. The learned, taking refuge in absorbing
Talmudic study, often were able to find in it forgetfulness
of the dreary sordidness and physical wretchedness in which
they were plunged. Israel Baal Shem Tov's Hasidism, "pietism," with its emphasis on joy, love, religious enthusiasm and
mystic communion with God, opened the heavens and illuminated and exalted the simplest of men. The Hasidic
element in Judaism emphasizes contemplative devotion and
enthusiasm in prayer. It stresses that religious ritual must

never be allowed to become a mechanical exercise; it must always be an aspiration to bring finite man into closer relation with the infinite God.

Characteristic of this is the song affectionately known by the name of A Dudale.

> Lord of the universe,
> I would sing You a song.
> Where can I find You,
> And where can I not find You?
> Wherever I go there are You,
> Wherever I stay there are You,
> Only You, You, You, You.
>   If good comes, there are You,
> And if, Heaven forfend, trouble comes,
> There are You, You, You, You, You.
>   You are, You were, You will be,
> You, You, You.
> In heaven and on earth, there are You,
> On high, below, there are You,
> You, You, You, You, You.
>   Wherever I may go,
> There are You.

Hasidism emphasizes that religion must not be chillingly solemn. It must be joyous and characterized by good cheer. Sorrow darkens the soul. Therefore worship must not be preoccupied with the thought of fear and sin; it can be expressed through blissful song, and even the rhythmic lilt of dance-like movements.

This emotional emphasis complements the intellectual emphasis in Judaism. Because of a happy balance between these two, Judaism knows nothing of either dervish-like frenzy or Yogi-like disciplinary austerity and exercises in posture, abnormal regulation of breathing, fasting, and self-hypnotism. It has never given itself to world-fleeing rapt contemplation in the effort to attain a trancelike ecstasy with utter apathy and indifference to pleasure or pain and all human desires and happenings. In Jewish life faith must be controlled by reason, while reason must be illuminated by faith. The truest wisdom is what the Bible calls wisdom of the heart.

Honoring equally mind, spirit, and soul, harmoniously united in communion with God, Judaism has given me guidance, strength, and light when in the world in which we live questionings have been deepest. I am grateful for my faith in which peace of soul and peace of mind are one.

EIGHT

CREED AND LIFE

THE quintessence of Judaism is contained in the words of Deuteronomy (6:4), "Hear, O Israel, the Lord is our God, the Lord is one." Beyond this declaration of faith there is in the religion of the Jew comparatively little of a creedal character. Judaism is primarily not a dogma or a creed, but a system of living characterized by ceremonial traditions, laws, regulations and customs expressive of ethical and historic folkways. It comprehends the whole sweep of life. An ancient custom of reading the Ten Commandments daily in synagogue was formally abolished lest anyone should get the impression that their cardinal authority covered the whole of Jewish belief and obligation.

Judaism is concerned first and foremost with works. It judges man by his conduct without inquiring into his beliefs. There is no catechism to which a Jew must subscribe at his Bar Mitzvah or when he joins a synagogue. Neither in the Torah of Moses nor the Bible as a whole nor the Talmud do we find a formulation of creed. The excommunications of Spinoza and Uriel Acosta are rare and dramatic exceptions in Jewish history.

Yet Judaism is not "all things to all men." It has its own
distinctive philosophy and theology. At times under the
pressure of interreligious disputations rabbis have attempted
to formulate the fundamental beliefs of the Jewish faith. The
best known summation was made in the twelfth century by
Moses Maimonides. However, the thirteen articles he set
down never became a test for defining what is a Jew. They do
not constitute an official authoritative canon of Jewish
belief. Put into poetic form they have entered the liturgy as a
hymn recited among the opening prayers of the day and
chanted in closing the Sabbath eve service. The Jew walking
through the quieted ghetto streets to his Sabbath-lit home
must often have hummed echoes of this closing hymn, a
profession of faith that gave him strength and comfort.

The first five principles enunciated by Maimonides attempt
to define the concept of God who was, who is, and who ever
will be. God is the God of the universe and of all living.
There is but one God. The third reinforces these affirmations.
It declares that God has no bodily form. In Judaism God
never has been and never can be associated with any human
figure. As the second commandment given at Mount Sinai
so strongly enjoins, there may be no attempts at creating any
physical images of the supremely spiritual concept of the
Divinity, whatever be the limitations of the human language
we needs must use to express the divine. When the Bible
speaks of man being created in the image of God it is using
very understandable terms to intimate abstractions conceived within the soul of man. Such phrases as the hand of
God, or God spoke, or references to Him as our Father, or
the Lord is my shepherd, are symbolically used terms which
seek to substantiate our spiritual intuitions. That the Torah
speaks in the language of men is recognized in all Jewish
teaching. But qualifying this is the basic and commanding

principle that the existence of God is above humanizing interpretation.

Among the terms of adoration of the Divine in Jewish prayer we find the name the Eternal, Omnipresent, Creator, Ruler of the Universe, Lord of the Universe, Glory of the Universe. These appellations reveal a cosmic religious outlook. The Bible, though it runs the gamut of human terminology, gives us deep intimations of infinity. It does not portray God as a glorified human being dwelling on an all-too-human Jewish Olympus. Moses, when he was first called, asked God to reveal His name and nature—"Behold, I come to the children of Israel and shall say to them the God of your fathers has sent me to you, and they shall say to me, 'What is His name?' What shall I say to them?" Then God revealed His name to Moses as "I am that I am," the Eternal Ever Existent (Exodus 3:13, 14). God's nature is the eternal spirit of the universe, existent before time began, existing after time shall be no more.

A primary and distinctive teaching of Judaism is that no human figure can be a unique manifestation of the Deity. Jews have not deified their seers however sanctified may have been their teachings. The religious revelation has been transmitted not by any single individual but by a long unbroken chain of men whose lives have been touched by the vision of the divine. While the Torah was given to the children of Israel through Moses, the Bible does not gloss over his weaknesses, or the faltering of any prophet, king or leader. On the Passover when the story of the redemption and the exodus from Egyptian slavery is told in Jewish homes, strikingly enough the name of Moses is mentioned but once. Moses is known in Jewish tradition as "Moses our teacher." He headed no hierarchy. There are no pilgrimages to his sepulchre. His place of burial remains unknown. Jehudah

Halevi (twelfth century) succinctly states that "the Jews did
not receive their eminence from Moses, but Moses received
his because of them." In a word, God who can be thought
of in no human figure, can be recognized and approached by
every individual without intermediary. He is "nigh to all
who call upon Him, to all who call upon Him in truth"
(Psalm 145:18).

In the fourth and fifth articles Maimonides states as did
the prophet Isaiah (41:4) that God the Eternal is the first and
the last, and that only He may be worshiped. The next four
define God's revelation: that all the words of His prophets
are true, that Moses was the greatest of all the prophets,
that the Torah which we have is that which was given to
Moses by God, and that it will never be changed nor will
He give another.

The next two credos are concerned with man's relation
to God. They state that God knows all our actions and our
thoughts, as the Psalmist declares (33:15), "He who forms the
heart of them all . . . understands all their works." He
rewards those who keep His commandments and punishes
those who disobey them.

The last two declarations deal with ultimates. The Messiah will come. The dead will be revived when God pleases.
The Bible while expressing faith in the immortality of the
soul says almost nothing about a heaven or a hell in the hereafter. To Job's question (14:14) "If a man die shall he live
again?" the Psalmist gives the answer (Psalm 88:13, 94:17)
that Sheol, the nether world of the grave, "the land of for-
getting," "the land of silence," does not annihilate the
human personality. That lives on beyond the grave. "Your
dead shall live again, the mortal being shall rise up; O
dwellers in the dust, awake and sing for joy" (Isaiah 26:19).
The Psalmist rhapsodically sings (139:7, 8), "Whither shall
I go from Thy spirit? Or whither shall I flee from Thy

presence? If I ascend unto heaven, Thou art there; if I make my bed in the nether world, behold Thou art there." Of old the Sadducees held that death spelt the end, but the Pharisees strongly maintained their belief in life after death and in the resurrection of the dead.

Not infrequently the Jew has thought and spoken of a physical heaven or hell awaiting one after death; but classic Jewish teaching more generally conceives of them not as places but as abstract states of existence. The rabbis declare that in the heavenly life to come there will be no physical eating or drinking, no begetting of children, no jealousy, no hatred, no strife, but there will be the bliss of enjoying the glory of the Divine Presence, for "the dust returns to the earth as it was, and the spirit to God who gave it" (Ecclesiastes 12:7), and "when I awake I shall be satisfied with Thy likeness" (Psalm 17:15).

Rabbi Jacob expressed a true sense of Jewish values when he said that this world is like a vestibule to the future world, and we must prepare ourselves in the vestibule so that we may enter the great reception hall. Yet, he said, better is one hour of penitence and good deeds in this world than all the life of the world to come, and paradoxically he added that better is one hour of spiritual repose in the world to come than all the life of this world. Clearly there was no dogmatically established representation of life after death. In Jewish thought, heaven is the attainment of spiritual fulfilment, and hell the exclusion from it. There is no fear that the grave will end the soul's communion with God. "I know that my Redeemer liveth, and that He will witness at the last upon the dust, and when after my skin this is destroyed, then without my flesh I shall see God" (Job 19:25, 26).

The daily morning prayers open with the affirmation that the God-given soul is pure, and with the assurance that just as we have awakened from sleep to new life on earth, so when the last sleep comes we shall awaken to new life in the world to come. This is a doctrine of faith that binds one to the Deity. It holds out the hope that death is not the end, and brings into daily life possibilities of beauty, sanctity, and inspiration of the infinite.

NINE

THE SYNAGOGUE

HILLEL, greatest of the rabbis of old, affirmed that God says "if you will come to My house, I will come to yours." The synagogue is man's house for God. It is a house of prayer. Its forms of worship and associations complement and invigorate the ordinary patterns of life.

Like other fundamental elements of Judaism, the synagogue goes back to the early days of Jewish history. It is a living symbol of its continuity. When I enter a synagogue I am deeply moved by the memories enshrined within it. I sense the mystic echoing of four thousand years of prayer. It is to me a living organism, the very body of the Jewish people. It harks back to the shrine of worship which the patriarch Jacob dedicated at Bethel—a name meaning "house of God" (Genesis 28:19). It is an integral development from the simple portable tabernacle built by the children of Israel in their desert wanderings from Egypt toward the Promised Land, the tabernacle which later became the grandiose Temple built by King Solomon.

In Biblical days the Temple in Jerusalem was the awesome fane of the whole nation. Eventually it was only there that sacrifice was authorized. To it religious pilgrimages were made from all over the country three times a year, at the spring, the summer and the autumn agricultural harvest festivals. In addition to the uniqueness and commanding eminence of the central Temple, there was a need for more intimate local sanctuaries where the people could more frequently gather and find at all times the fulfilment of worship in their personal prayer. As a result, not competing with but complementing the national worship in the Temple of Jerusalem the synagogue grew up. We still hear the anguished cry of the Psalmist (74:8) after an invasion when looking on the ruins of such synagogues he wept that "they had burned all the meeting places of God in the land."

The conquest of the country by Babylon in the year 586 B.C.E. meant exile for many of its people and the destruction of the Temple and of the synagogues. Then, twenty-five hundred years ago, there began the active development of the synagogue as we know it. It was a consoling reflex of the destroyed Temple in Jerusalem. Through the prophet Ezekiel (11:16) the divine word came to the exiles in Babylon saying, "I have become for them a small sanctuary in the lands to which they have come."

Morning and afternoon, the set times of the daily services in Zion's Temple, became the times when the exiles gathered for prayer in these small sanctuaries. There was good authority for making prayer take the place held formerly by the ritual of sacrifice. Long since the prophet Hosea had called on the people (14:3), "Take with you words and return to the Lord . . . so shall we substitute the prayer of our lips for the sacrifice of bulls." This substitution was to become the primary function of the synagogue which grew up in the exile in Babylon.

With the return to the Land of Israel after that exile, synagogues supplementing the official national Temple sprang up anew, both in Jerusalem and throughout the country. How numerous they were is clearly indicated in the New Testament. Almost nineteen centuries ago, ruin again descended upon the central Temple in the Holy City when the mighty armies of Rome utterly destroyed it. Then the synagogue inevitably took on enhanced meaning, both in the devastated homeland and in the diaspora, blossoming and growing in strength and comforting a people bereaved.

But the Temple was not forgotten, and the longing for it never ceased. In its very structure the synagogue has been "oriented" so that the worshiper faces toward the site of the Temple's holy of holies in ancient Jerusalem. This makes all who stand in prayer in a synagogue at one with their forebears, even unto the day three thousand years ago when King Solomon dedicated the majestic Temple of which his father, David, had dreamed. He entreated the Lord to hearken to any of his people, wheresoever they might be, as they "pray unto Thee toward their land which Thou gavest unto their fathers, the city which Thou hast chosen and the house which I have built for Thy name" (I Kings 8:46–49). In facing toward Mount Zion in prayer one is united not only with King Solomon but also with Daniel in Babylon. We are told (Daniel 6:11) that three times daily he prayed while turning toward Jerusalem. Such cumulative memories press themselves upon me and thrill me when I enter a synagogue, and they give to my prayer stirringly meaningful associations.

For the most part calm simplicity characterized the architecture of the historic synagogue. In keeping with the second commandment, statues, images, or pictures are strictly excluded as figures that might lead to idolatry. The altar of the ancient Temple is represented by the Ark, where handwritten parchment scrolls of the Pentateuch are ceremoniously enshrined. Each scroll, placed upright, is protected by an enveloping mantle, and is adorned with a silver crown or bells. Before the Ark hangs an ever-burning light, recalling the light which the priests always kept burning in the Temple of old.

No priests are required for the conduct of the services. On special occasions, the "Cohens," lineal descendants of the Biblical priesthood through the line of Aaron, bless the congregation as did their ancestors. A "Cohen" is also privileged to be first, and a "Levy" second, of those called to the public reading of the Torah. For the rest, the congregants share in the service as members of "a kingdom of priests." The exercise of religious duties is an obligation which rests equally on all the children of Israel. There is no priestly caste, and there are no special duties or prerogatives that belong to a rabbi over and above the congregants. In the traditional architecture of the synagogue the official reading desk is not placed on a platform from which a cleric might conduct the service for a congregation assembled before him. It is set in the center area of the building so that all may the better hear and participate in the service.

One functionary may be said to lead in the service—the hazzan. A hazzan is not a member of any pontifical profession. He is a layman who, musically endowed, can chant acceptably and lead the congregation's chanting. Any Jew of good character and with the necessary Hebrew learning and vocal ability may be "the representative of the congregation" as the hazzan is called in Hebrew. Though in English he is usually known as a cantor, his essential function is not to be a soloist displaying his vocal gifts before a muted listening audience that is limited to giving responses and joining in occasional hymns. The hazzan reads the selection from the Torah scroll, and an individual congregant is given the honor of chanting from the prophetic or historic books of the Bible.

For the rest, the prayers are sung by the congregation as a whole under the leadership of the hazzan.

The service is traditionally conducted with the emotional warmth and joy of song. It is true that the Amidah, central prayer in each service, is read by the congregants in silent devotion; but it is then repeated by the hazzan with its traditional cantillation. The synagogue chants are as a rule ancient and varied. They are charged with the associations of the festal or solemn character of the day and the emotional content of the prayer itself. But synagogal music is not ritually prescribed and unchangeable, and original compositions are not infrequently heard. According to many musicologists, the song of Moses at the crossing of the Red Sea is sung in my Congregation Shearith Israel to a chant that goes back to Bible times. The Psalmist (98:1) said, "Sing to the Lord a new song." In modern times there has been a marked tendency to revive his words. Striking variety has been given to the musical character of the services by the setting of prayers and hymns to new melodies.

There was a powerful organ in the ancient Temple in Jerusalem. But after the destruction of that Temple all instrumental music was excluded from synagogue services as a sign of mourning. This gives to the cantor and the choir the responsibility of assuring unity and harmony in the congregational singing of hymns.

Many customs, some of them going back to Biblical days, give added color and character to the synagogue. Thus, one should hasten to the house of prayer even on the Sabbath when relaxation and repose permeate every aspect of the day; but on leaving he should walk with leisurely pace, unless he is proceeding to the house of study. Before entering the synagogue hands are washed even as the Psalmist declared (26:6) that he would wash his hands in purity before going about the altar. At the entrance one says with the Psalmist

(5:8), "In the abundance of Thy lovingkindness I will enter
Thy house; I will bow toward Thy holy Temple in reverence
of Thee." One then proceeds to his regular seat. There often
develops great attachment for that seat, the more so when
it has been formerly occupied by one's father and grandfather.
It has been for me a moving experience reviving the past to
take my place in the venerable candle-lit synagogue in
London where my forebears sat. I can well understand my
congregants who cling with unshakable sentiment to the
location in their present building corresponding with that
associated with their families in our older synagogues, revert-
ing even to pre-Revolutionary days.

For morning prayers the worshiper enwraps himself in a
talleth, a white prayer shawl, with fringes on each corner.
In Biblical days the officiating priests wore a miter or turban
"for glory and beauty" (Exodus 28:40). The tradition of
head-covering goes back to that august memory. Prayers are
recited standing or sitting. The custom of kneeling to which
the Bible bears witness has given place to reverent bowing.

The congregational participation in the service combines
spontaneity with set forms, and warmth with decorum. It
is the proud tradition of my synagogue that through its three
centuries of worship in the New World it has achieved and
exemplified an inspiring union between the free movement
of the spirit in personal devotions, and the impressive stateli-
ness which should mark congregational prayer.

"Let them make Me a sanctuary that I may dwell among
them"(Exodus 25:8). The primary function of the synagogue
is to provide a meeting place for communal worship. It is
not a cloistered chapel or a confessional shrine. A complete
religious service cannot be held unless there is present a
congregation consisting of a minimum of ten Jewish men.
A lad becomes qualified to be counted for this needed quorum
when he attains the age of thirteen years. No confirmation or

examination in creed is required of him. On reaching that age he automatically becomes a Bar Mitzvah, that is "a son of commandment," and upon him henceforth rests responsibility in Jewish life. Theoretically this comes of itself with entrance into teen age. But this important transition into community membership is marked by preliminary study, by participation in the reading of the Torah, and festivity in celebration of the occasion.

Women and girls are not counted in making up the religious quorum. The historic reason for this is found in the popular phrases that woman's place is in the home and woman's work is never done. We need only recall some features in the picture of the ideal wife painted in Proverbs (31:15, 27): "She rises while it is yet night and gives food to her household and a portion to her maidens. . . . She looks well to the ways of her household, she eats not the bread of idleness." She weaves, she sews, and engages in many other activities mentioned in that glowing description. Because of such obligations, especially those called for in the care of young children, she may not be free to attend synagogue services at a set time. Men and boys ordinarily are not tied down by such exacting home and family duties.

To minimize possible distractions which might disturb religious devotion and concentration in prayer women and men have been seated separately in the historic synagogue. This custom goes back two thousand years to the Temple in Jerusalem. It was found that on occasions such as the joyous religious festival of drawing water, frivolity unbecoming the Temple sanctity was hard to avoid. The priests then made the regulation that the men and the women should be separated from one another at communal worship. Separation of the sexes is a characterisic feature in the concept of chastity which plays so important a part in Jewish life.

The congregational *minyan*, the nucleus of ten men for

the holding of a complete service in effect gives to the
individual a sense of importance in that he is "counted for
minyan." The emotion of prayer is a contagious one, and
joint prayer stimulates the spirit of worship. One of the
rabbis said that where ten or more pray together, there God's
presence, His Shechinah, is to be found and felt among them.
In counting for *minyan* there is absolute and undeviating
equality of all Jews, the lowliest and the greatest, the richest
and the poorest. Each is one.

The synagogue as a corporate body is autonomous. Affiliation with associations of similar religious outlook is entirely
voluntary. A Jewish congregation is not subject to religious
control by any ecclesiastical organization or pontifical body.

In Hebrew the synagogue is called *beth hakeneseth,* the
house of assembly, the gathering place. This term was translated literally into ancient Greek as *synagogé* (assembly),
and under that name it entered into modern languages. For
nineteen centuries the synagogue has been the supreme cohesive force that has brought and held Jews together. It is
the central rallying point for community prayer, the forum
for democratic thinking and action, and the pulpit for the
definition of communal duty and the resolving of community
problems. It has been the primary organic unit of Jewish
communal self-expression. It has been the center where
prayer and religious idealism have united to guide action
both by the individual and by the organized community. It
has been the place where the Jewish poor found help and the
stranger found hospitality. To the synagogue came individuals
seeking a rabbinic court to settle their differences. Today it
is also the Jewish social center where men's clubs, sister-
hoods and youth groups gather for social, communal, educa-
tional, as well as religious activity.

Most striking is the synagogue's central position in education. This has been continuous in all lands and all ages.

Even on the Sabbath this education goes on, and it is not considered to be in conflict with the command to rest. In ancient Alexandria, Philo said, "Jews occupy themselves every seventh day with the philosophy of their fathers, dedicating that time to the acquisition of knowledge and the study of the truths of nature." The popular name which is generally given to a synagogue is "Schul" (school), for to it children have gone for instruction, not once but four, or five, or even six days a week. They are taught to read and understand their prayers and the Torah, often with the Hebrew commentary of that keen medieval French scholar, Rashi, the Bible story, and something of the whole history of the Jewish people, as well as the ritual and ceremonies of Jewish life.

When books were costly and rare, it was to the synagogue that one would go to find books of learning such as volumes of the Talmud and commentaries on the Bible. Adults continued to come to the "Schul," whether singly or in groups, for personal study. The great rabbi Hillel remarked that an ignoramus cannot be truly pious. Religious education of the adult has not been limited to a weekly sermon interpreting some Biblical teaching or discussing some problem of living. The Talmud counsels a man when his day's work is done to drop in at the synagogue, pause there for brief study of the Bible or some rabbinic work, recite his afternoon prayers, and then continue on his way home. If he goes straight home, the Talmud opines, when he gets there he may wearily drop asleep and neglect his religious obligation of daily study and prayer. Jewish study is not for children only; all must regard it as a constant and continuous life-long obligation in which to glory.

There is a rabbinic saying that greater is Torah than the priesthood or royalty, for the priesthood requires twenty-four qualifications and royalty thirty, while the Torah calls for forty-eight, to wit: study, hearkening of the ear, ordering of the lips, understanding, and insight of the heart, awe, reverence, humility, joyousness, association with sages, consorting with fellow students, discussion with pupils, steadiness in study of the Bible and Mishnah, minimizing business, minimizing worldly interests, minimizing indulgence, minimizing sleep, minimizing converse, minimizing jocosity, patience, a good heart, faith in the sages, acceptance of chastisements, knowing one's place, rejoicing in one's lot, setting a limit to one's words, not claiming merit for oneself, being beloved, loving God, loving one's fellow men, loving the right course, loving rectitude, loving reproof, fleeing honor, not being arrogant in one's learning, not delighting to lay down the law, bearing the yoke with one's fellow student, judging him favorably, establishing him in the truth and in peace, pondering on one's study, questioning and answering, hearing and adding to what one hears, learning in order to teach, learning in order to practise, enlightening one's teacher, ordering well that which one hears, and repeating a saying in the name of him who said it. This exhaustive and perhaps exhausting program for learning has been centered in the synagogue. A commanding tradition in all Jewish communities, even primitive ones living among illiterate peoples, has been to have schooling freely available to all the children. Giving to a synagogue takes precedence over giving to charity; but the support of poor students to enable them to study the Torah is placed above the support of the synagogue. The obligation of constant religious study is regarded as more pressing for the religious life even than that of maintaining a house of prayer. Therefore synagogue funds may be used for religious education, but the converse is not permitted. To religious education goes all priority, and in the vivid dictum of the rabbis it may not be interrupted for the rebuilding of the Temple.

Placing education in a primary position has strengthened the synagogue and made it more surely the strategic bastion of Jewish survival. The world over it has been the most powerful cohesive Jewish force in a non-Jewish environment. On important days in the religious calendar Jews will come from scattered and remote outposts, often at great sacrifice, to meet with their brethren in religious partnership within the synagogue. In the past two millennia it has been the pivotal center of Jewish life for a people scattered over the face of the earth with no political state or authoritarian institutions to hold them together. Most potently it has impressed the character of a family kinship on a people reputedly composed of markedly individualistic personalities.

The synagogue has been the symbol of the continuity of the Jewish people. It has been the traditional center of the distinctive Jewish culture and learning which are the abundant fruitage of the Bible. It has linked the Jew to his people by a bond stronger than that of blood and nobler than flight from anti-Semitism. The synagogue is the symbol of my Judaism and all that it means to me that I am a Jew. It is more influential in making and in keeping me a Jew than the chance of my birth from Jewish parents.

The synagogue is a house of prayer, a school for the young, a college for the adult, a center for the sanctification of the Bar Mitzvah and of the hallowing of the wedding day and other personal joys, it is the shrine of comfort in sorrow, the inspirer of Jewish communal service, the constant reminder of the promised redemption of Zion—in a word the nucleating meeting place, transmitter and invigorator of all that is best in Jewish life. The Jew in his synagogue bears witness and renews his loyalty to the ideals which are his to uphold. Jews whose lives are not quickened by the synagogue cannot understand what the Psalmist said (Psalm 84:5) "Happy are they who dwell in Thy house."

TEN

PRAYER

THEY who gave the world the Book of Psalms have been a people of prayer. This the rabbis define as worship by the heart. It is not so much petition as it is the bringing of man into harmony with the universal spirit by attuning the soul to communion with God. The Hasidim who stress the mystic element in Judaism accentuate the fact that prayer is the instrument for union with the Shechinah, the divine presence. "I will sing to the Lord while I live, I will sing praise to my God while I have my being" (Psalm 104:33, 34) is a true expression of Jewish faith.

It is a psychological necessity and usual practise to set fixed times for prayer in addition to the spontaneous calls for outpouring of the soul. Any time may be no time. Worldly pressures too often compete successfully with the inclination to pray. Sometimes a pious devotee may go to excess, neglect his worldly duties, and give too much time to his devotions. Judaism set definite times for prayer, not only on Sabbath and other special days, but every day in the year, thrice daily, morning, afternoon and evening. In addition, a pious

Jew will find a hundred occasions every day in which to thank God for His blessings.

The Hebrew prayer book contains the liturgy for weekdays, Sabbaths, festivals and holy days, and also occasional prayers from awakening in the morning to just before closing the eyes for sleep at night. Developed organically from the Psalms which were chanted in the Temple in Jerusalem, the prayer book of today includes more than half of those Psalms. Through innumerable phrases, verses and paragraphs, the words, the thoughts and the affirmations of the Bible are woven into its texture. When the canon of the Bible was closed, more than two thousand years ago, the Jewish soul continued to speak and to sing in creative spiritual beauty. The prayer book has preserved and transmitted eclectically from generation to generation the classic quintessence of Judaism's exalted praying, expressing the conscience and the soul of the whole people.

The duty of praying rests equally on all, rabbi, priest, and layman alike. Jewish prayer expresses the soul, the faith, and the outcry of the heart of the whole community. It is very largely set in the plural. The welfare of the individual yields to the needs of the community as a whole. On the Day of Atonement the high priest would pray in the Temple that a traveler's prayer for dry weather might not be heard when the community is praying for the rain needed by the crops in the fields. In Jewish thought one who prays but for himself is regarded as one who withdraws into his own house and does not assist his fellows in meeting the general needs. The traditional prayer book gives constant expression to the collective social character of Jewish idealism. Yet it does not overlook the instinctive aspiration for individual saintliness. It has served through the ages as a manual of intense personal devotion and piety. But it realizes the limitations of a self-centered, cloistered virtue. In giving expression to the ideal of achieving an ennobled society, it becomes primarily the community's prayer book. Because of this, the individual draws inspiration and strength from his fellows, while in his turn he adds his increment of warmth and spirit to the general fervor. The unit of a spiritualized society becomes a congregation assembled for united worship, for affirmation of its ideals, and resolve to attain them.

God's kingdom on earth is destined not for the elect few, but for the blessing of all. In the Talmud the question is asked, what is the meaning of the phrase "in an acceptable time" in the Psalmist's words (69:14) "as for me, let my prayer come to Thee, O Lord, in an acceptable time." The answer given is that when prayer is offered together with a congregation it is in an acceptable time.

Prayer may be long or short. When Moses besought healing for Miriam (Numbers 12:13) he uttered but five intense Hebrew monosyllables, *"El na r'fa na lah,"* "God, I pray heal her." We are also told that when supplicating for his people he prayed for forty days and forty nights (Deuteronomy 9:18, 25). The contrast lends itself to a volume of interpretation. The variety of prayer parallels the variety of religious experience. Pious Jews of old would sit in silent contemplation for an hour before the beginning of a formal synagogue service. Devotion may be intensified by such contemplative silence, just as it may be stimulated by utterance.

Characteristic of prayer in Judaism is the acceptance of the fact that it may be answered, not that it must be answered. The petitioner cannot command. The phrase "May it be Thy will" constantly recurs. This thought is deeply rooted. It is told of a well-known Hasidic rabbi to whom misfortunes came that when his wife asked him to pray for relief, he replied, "I spend my life trying to do the will of God. Shall I now ask Him to do my will?"

The rabbis teach that one should not pray for a miracle.

They emphasize that it is vain to pray for averting or nullifying that which is already determined, inescapable, or inevitable. Thus if a woman be with child, to pray that the child may be a son is a vain prayer, for the sex of the infant is already established. Or, they say, if a man on his way hears that a riot has taken place in his town, to pray that the disturbance should not have affected his own home is a vain prayer, for its damage or escape has already been determined.

Above all, the principle is stressed that prayer may not be a substitute for action. It must strengthen resolve, clarify thought, and guide conduct. In sickness prayer for healing must be an adjunct to the resources which medical knowledge can bring to bear. The rabbis who found in the Bible illustrations for every teaching recall that when in the exodus from Egypt the children of Israel found themselves caught between the waters of the Red Sea and the pursuing Egyptian army, God said to Moses (Exodus 14:15), "Wherefore do you cry unto Me? Speak to the children of Israel that they go forward."

Moreover, Judaism emphasizes that prayer must be united with moral living. The Book of Proverbs (28:9) forthrightly declares, "He who turns his ear away from hearkening to religious teaching even his prayer is an abomination." We may ask God to operate only when we cooperate. Prayer cannot silence wrongdoing, but wrongdoing can silence prayer. An ancient Jewish tradition gives an individual the right to close the synagogue of a whole community so long as a glaring and remediable personal wrong is not corrected. For example, if a man refuse to support his old and needy father, the father may get up in the synagogue and state his case, and no further public prayers may be conducted in that synagogue until the congregation as a whole has seen to it that the wrong is righted.

As the Jew trudged forward through the leaden-footed centuries, he found that his book of prayers on the one hand expressed his unconquerable religious faith, and on the other that it was a high refuge against the man-made cataclysms of history. The prayer book allows for no despair. Vibrantly and constantly it expresses the hope for the Redeemer promised by the prophets, and for Israel's renascence in its own Promised Land. It confirms the Jew in his faith that he shall yet be comforted for the sorrows he has borne as the suffering servant of mankind, and that once more "from Zion shall go forth God's teaching and the word of the Lord from Jerusalem" (Isaiah 2:3).

This fervent and boundless hope running through the whole prayer book is not an expression of an assertive self-righteous nationalism. It is the yearning for mankind's spiritual healing by divine light. God is addressed not only as "our God and God of our fathers," but most often as "Ruler of the universe" or "universal Lord." Virtually every blessing is offered to the "Lord our God, Ruler of the universe." The prayer for peace on earth is the climax of Israel's greatest prayers. Every one of the three daily synagogue services closes with the aspiration for the day when wickedness and oppression shall be overcome, when all the children of men shall invoke God, and all earth-dwellers will honor Him and recognize and accept His sovereignty. It is the prayer for the Messianic day when all men shall live together in social comity and world brotherhood, when there will be the fulfilment of the vision of the prophet that "The Lord shall be King over all the earth; on that day the Lord shall be One and His name One" (Zechariah 14:9).

The predominant note of the prayer book is the adoration of God. It is characterized by sustained and ecstatic blessing and praise of God far more than by petition. In paeans of soaring rhapsody born of the Biblical Psalms there pour forth praises of God's justice tempered by His mercy, His righteousness conjoined with His love, His strength united with His compassion. It is a book of praise rather than a book of beseeching. Page after page is given up to an exultant adoration of God as man's infinite ideal.

Thus in Jewish tradition prayer becomes a joyous spiritual exercise. It is essentially the expression of thanksgiving for the privileges of life. From Talmudic times the opening prayers of the daily morning service have been blessings, both of the reawakening of the soul in purity, and for all the physical phenomena of living.

One ancient prayer stands out prominently in the consciousness of the Jew. It is called the Kaddish, "holy," and we find it quoted in the first phrases of the Paternoster. It is written in Aramaic, the vernacular used in the Holy Land two thousand years ago. As a closing prayer it marks the completion of the main sections in a service. It looks to God's will being done and the coming of His kingdom speedily in our days. The essence of the Kaddish is found in the word, "Exalted and hallowed be God's great name in this world of His creation. May His will be fulfilled by the revelation of His sovereignty in your lifetime and in the life of the whole house of Israel, speedily and soon . . . Be His great name blessed forever, yea, throughout eternity . . . beyond the power of all blessings, hymns, and consolations of this world to express." The whole compass of spiritual bliss is invoked in such additional paragraphs as "May peace abundant descend from heaven, with life and plenty, healing solace, liberation, rescue and deliverance, atonement and forgiveness, redemption and salvation, for us and all Thy people Israel . . . May He who creates the harmony of the spheres, in His tender love create peace for us and for all Israel."

Over the centuries the Kaddish has come to be recited in

synagogue, or wherever a *minyan* of ten men may gather, by a mourner during the first eleven months of his bereavement, and on the anniversaries of the death of any close of kin. Yet it is not a plaint about the finality of death, nor does it directly or indirectly mention death. The mourner does not look backward to sorrow but forward to the hope that all men may know peace and new life through the hallowing of God's name in the world with the coming of His kingdom. It is a prayer in keeping with the sentiment of the rabbis of old who declared that one should not stand up to pray in a spirit of sadness but rather with the desire to help fulfil the divine will.

Need it be added that the rabbis constantly enjoin the worshiper devoutly to ponder both in his mind and his heart the meaning of the words which cross his lips? They stress that one must strive to remove all thoughts that would distract concentrated devotion. Man must feel that his praying brings him into God's presence. If he were speaking before an earthly king he would order his words as carefully as possible; how much the more will he strive to do this when standing before the King of kings, the Holy One, blessed be He. Prayer without this concentrated devotion is likened to body without soul.

It is further emphasized that prayer must be a combination of spirit and mind. Devotional warmth, inspiration, and ecstasy must not lead to irrationalism and to deviations into nebulous paths of excessive emotion or unrealistic mysticism. Frank and brave questions of the mind must be recognized no less than the mystic longings of the soul. The prayer book contains many selections from the Bible, from ethical and religious writings, the teachings and aphorisms of the rabbis, and directives for the priesthood in the Jerusalem Temple. Central in the synagogue morning services on Monday and Thursday, on the Sabbath both morning and afternoon, on

all festivals and on special days in the Jewish calendar, is the
reading from the Torah—a word, let us remind ourselves,
which means instruction, teaching.

The primary concern of Jewish prayer is with ethical and
spiritual ideals of living rather than with abstract theological
dogma. Yet there has often been added to the morning
service or to the Sabbath eve service a medieval hymn, Yigdal,
summarizing the credo of Judaism as formulated by Maimonides in thirteen principles. This is the nearest approach to
a creedal text, and it is a comparatively late addition to the
liturgy. The only synagogal affirmation of faith, and one
that is essential in every morning and evening service of
prayer, is the recitation of the Shema, the six Hebrew words
which make up the fourth verse in the sixth chapter of the
Biblical Book of Deuteronomy, "Hear, O Israel, the Lord
is our God, the Lord is one." Every morning in his prayers
the Jew declares his spiritual happiness:—"Happy are we!
How goodly is our portion, how pleasant our lot, how beautiful our heritage! Happy are we who at early morn and at
evenfall twice each day with fervent love declare, Hear, O
Israel, the Lord is our God, the Lord is one."

The six brief and simple words declaring God's unity with
their vision of the universal God of all mankind summarize
Jewish belief. Within that framework no Jew is excluded
from the fellowship of faith. These six Hebrew words have
been the kernel of Jewish prayer. Nineteen hundred years
ago the historian Josephus declared that the custom of the
prayerful recitation of the Shema twice a day was instituted by
Moses himself. They are the first words of prayer taught
to the Jewish child as he passes on from lisping babyhood
and begins to speak, and they are the last words whispered
at night before one falls asleep, even as they are the final
prayer or last conscious words uttered at the deathbed. These
are the words which have been heroically proclaimed by

countless martyrs in their agony as the triumphant justification of their faith. The rabbis declare that because of their solemnity they may not be said in an unclean place, nor may the reading of them and the verses which follow them be interrupted even to return the salutation of a king. They must be read with reverence, devotion and awe. It is customary to close and cover the eyes when uttering the hallowed words so as to block out all visual distraction from the worshiper's devotion.

This all-motivating prayerful declaration of Jewish faith that there is but one universal God is followed in the prayer book as in the Bible by the words, "You shall love the Lord your God, with all your heart, and with all your soul, and with all your might," another fundamental of religious teaching. It is not so much the fear of God as the love of God which must ever be in one's heart and soul. It is a constant theme in Jewish teaching that you must live "to *love* the Lord your God, to hearken to His voice, and cleave to Him, for that is your life and the length of your days." "You shall *love* the Lord your God and keep His . . . commandments always" (Deuteronomy 30:20; 11:1).

Then the Shema continues, "These words which I command you this day shall be in your heart. And you shall teach them diligently to your children." The teaching of children must not be interrupted say the rabbis even for rebuilding the Temple, for the world rests upon their breath. The Talmud asks the question who is ignorant, only to give the subtle answer the one who does not educate his children. When all our children shall be taught of the Lord great shall be their peace, says the prophet Isaiah (54:13). Judaism with its universal message is a culture which has to be purposively transmitted. We are told in the Talmud that Jerusalem had no less than three hundred and ninety-four schools before its destruction by the Romans. According to the standards set up by the rabbis, Jews everywhere, even in days when the great mass of mankind was illiterate, were bound to appoint teachers for the young. A community which engaged no teacher could be put under a ban until one was employed.

The Shema, that fundamental prayer, goes on to call for an ever-present concern with the words of God, "when you sit in your home, when you walk on the way, when you lie down, and when you rise up." Being a Jew is something that comes to expression not only at set times of formal prayer, but also in every aspect of life, in the home, in business, in the market, everywhere and at all times. The Shema then enjoins that God's word be bound to your hand, and be as frontlets between your eyes. Symbols of complete acceptance of this are the tefillin (phylacteries), two small square black leather cases in which are sealed Biblical passages written on parchment. Through these one literally binds God's words on his hand and between his eyes during his weekday morning prayers. But the words of God must remain with him when these visible symbols are removed after the completion of his prayers. He also affixes to his doorpost a mezuzah, a small parchment scroll containing the words of the Shema, thus fulfilling the command "You shall write them upon the doorposts of your house and upon your gates."

These verses four to nine in the sixth chapter of Deuteronomy constitute the nuclear heart of Jewish praying. They are followed by the reading of Deuteronomy 11:13–21, developing the theme of the Shema in terms of the relation of conduct to life. This is then followed by Numbers 15:37–41 which calls for the Jewish uniform of the tsitsith, "fringe," the fringed garment worn by men under the shirt, and the talleth, the fringed prayer shawl worn during morning prayers. "And it shall be to you a fringe that you may look upon and remember all the commandments and do them.

Then you will not stray after your heart and your eyes"
(Numbers 15:39). It is not only a clerical priesthood which
is vested in robes bearing symbolic insignia of a religious
ministry. To every man belongs the talleth, the white garment
of purity. Enveloping him physically, spiritually it helps
shut out the material world and create a mood of its own in
which the soul rises to the realm of prayer where the greatest
reserves of human strength reside. Prayer is not so much a
means to obtain one's desire as it is an ultimate source of
guidance and strength. It has its cardinal place in faith, and in
the story of the Jewish pilgrimage through the ages it has
been a light that fails not.

ELEVEN

SEMANTICS

WHAT is the language of the Jew? In Bible days it was Hebrew, and it is once more Hebrew in the modern State of Israel. There was never a time in the interim when Hebrew disappeared from usage. As the language of the Bible, of prayer in the synagogue, and as the subject of intensive study in the school, it has remained up to modern times a lingua franca for Jews the world over. However, outside the realm of religion and literature the vernacular in the lands where the Jew lived ordinarily became the spoken and mother tongue.

In the medieval era, violent and sudden expulsions and mass migrations of Jews sometimes created a diaspora of language as well as of people with the development over the years of a specifically Judean dialect of the tongue which those who had escaped carried with them to the lands of refuge. The Jews driven from Spain in 1492 took with them their medieval Spanish. This language lived on actively in the Balkans for more than four centuries. Uprooted from its native soil, and with all contacts broken with Spain, it nevertheless kept its basic Spanish character unchanged while gradually becoming increasingly dialectic through added Jewish words and phrases. Judeo-Spanish, or Ladino as it is called, is written in Hebrew characters, and in it there has been produced a not inconsiderable literature.

After the Black Death in Europe in 1348–49, surviving Jews from Germany fled eastward from the horrors and massacres to which they were subjected. They took with them Middle High German, the language then spoken in Germany. Over the years this transported language became a distinctive Judean dialect known as Yiddish. Written in Hebrew characters, the only addition to its basic German vocabulary are some ten per cent of Hebrew words and about five per cent of words borrowed from environmental Slavonic languages such as Polish or Russian. In the United States Yiddish was used by large numbers of immigrants, particularly during the end of the nineteenth and the beginning of the twentieth century, and a large number of English words were absorbed into the language. Yet Yiddish has remained basically a dialect of medieval German. It has kept alive not a few words and forms which were used in old German but no longer occur in the modern German tongue.

Yiddish has contributed to Jewish life a rich literature including religious books, stories, poetry, fables, dramas, novels, magazines, and newspapers. On the American scene, modern writers whose works have been translated into English, such as Yehoash, S. Ansky, Isaac Loeb Peretz, Peretz Hirshbein, Sholom Aleichem, and Sholom Asch, have found an honored place in the story of American letters, and to this day some excellent poetry is being written in Yiddish in the United States. There are a number of Yiddish-speaking schools and academies of Jewish learning scattered through the country. Yiddish is still a vital linguistic force, and New York has taken the place of Vilna as the cultural center of the language for the American continent. Strikingly enough, the process of Americanization of Eastern European Jewish immigrants was actively furthered by the Yiddish press, and Yiddish speaking groups in organized labor contributed not a little to the sound upbuilding of the American labor movement. A recent polyglot dictionary which gives the words in seven world languages includes Yiddish as one of them. It is estimated that before the ruthless destruction of Eastern European Jewry in recent years the Yiddish language was spoken by no less than twelve million Jews. Today though displaced by Hebrew in Israel and for the most part by the vernacular elsewhere, it is still a vital cultural and social instrument of communication.

Very few, if any, consider the use of Yiddish or Ladino cardinal to being a Jew. The impermanence of these languages is accepted, and in Israel where strong emphasis is placed on the revived Hebrew tongue, the use of them is discouraged.

One cannot understand the full import of Judaism without knowledge of Hebrew. It is the language of the Jewish faith. I have worshiped in synagogues in forty-four countries in five continents, from Finland to New Zealand, from Turkey to Thailand, but I have never found myself a stranger unable to follow the service because of ignorance of the language current in the country. The service in Hebrew made me feel immediately at home and at one with my religious brethren everywhere, able to join in the prayers which for half a century I have led in my historic Shearith Israel Synagogue in New York. There is far-reaching truth in the Biblical story of the confusion of tongues at the Tower of Babel. Oneness of language is a potent unifying influence among men.

Hebrew unifies across time as it does geographically. One thrills to hear in the synagogue the reading of the Ten Commandments echoing the very words heard by the children of Israel as they stood at Mount Sinai. Week after week when

the section from the Pentateuch is chanted, time vanishes
and there is heard once more the voice of Moses speaking,
without an interpreter and without the changes of accentua-
tion and associations which a translation inevitably intro-
duces. When the selection from the prophets is read, we
hear each week anew the sounds that they heard within their
inmost soul millennia ago. When the Hebrew Psalms are
chanted, we can imagine ourselves in the glorious Temple
King Solomon built in Jerusalem as we listen to the very
words sung there by the Levitical choir. When the Cohens
of today, descendants of the Temple servitors, chant in the
synagogue the Biblical words of priestly blessing, a Jew must
feel at one with his ancestors of a hundred generations in
reverently hearkening to the sacred words. The Hebrew
language and the Hebrew language alone can express that
complete spiritual identification across the centuries. In every
generation their ancient tongue has been a bastion of kinship among the Jewish people. Though of course an individual may offer his personal prayers in the language that he
best understands, the traditional liturgy has been in the Hebrew language, for that alone completely expresses the
traditional aspirations, hopes and ideals of the Jewish people
of all ages in their pristine intent. Every language has its
own unique character. Martin Luther after struggling to
translate the Hebrew Bible into German declared that "the
words of the Hebrew tongue have a special energy. It is
impossible to convey so much so briefly in any other language." The subtleties of a language are indeed untranslat-
able. In a broad sense when Christianity translated Judaism
into Greek and Islam translated Judaism into Arabic, there
was involved a necessary change of emphasis from the original
revelation. Coverdale in translating the Bible tried to express
the meaning of the Hebrew word *hesed*. In doing this he
introduced into the English language the word lovingkindness

to suggest the associations of *hesed*: endearing love, kindness, goodness, pious devotion, pity, fidelity. Similarly the Hebrew word *rahamim* is almost always rendered in English by mercy, which however does not convey the full measure of tender compassionate love felt in the Hebrew. Likewise *tsedakah* is often translated by the English word charity, a word which does not exclude the suggestion of a patronising and perhaps even a humiliating giving. Such associations are completely absent from the Hebrew term *tsedakah* which basically means justice, righteousness, justice expressed through righteousness, a concept which puts the giving on a different level of ethical duty from that underlying the term charity.

The Christian world has added to its vocabulary many a Hebrew word such as Amen, hallelujah, hosanna, paradise, Sabbath, Messiah, Shechinah, shibboleth, jubilee, cherub, seraph, satan, shekel, mammon, hyssop, leviathan, manna, and kosher. The admission of such words into the English language has been necessitated by their virtual untranslatability. Often the associations of a translated word blur the focus of the Hebrew original. "Fear the Lord," the English translation of a recurring phrase in the Hebrew Bible, is very different from the Hebrew original which means to revere and stand in awe of the Lord.

Dwelling on the uniqueness of the original text of the Hebrew Bible in no wise is meant to belittle the English translations of the Bible which have made the English speaking world also peoples of the Book, and which have taken a distinguished place in the history of English literature. The religious thinking of millions who speak the English language has been lifted to the heights and immeasurably enriched by the English versions of the Bible. Many of the thoughts felicitously expressed both in Hebrew and in English have become proverbial, such as "put not your trust in princes," "the race is not to the swift," "pride goes before a fall," "how are the mighty fallen," "there is nothing new under the sun," "can the leopard change his spots," "the fleshpots of Egypt," "tell it not in Gath," "out of the mouth of babes and suck- lings," "take sweet counsel together," "a soft answer turns away wrath," "the apple of one's eye," "a still small voice," and numberless other Biblical phrases and sayings.

Difficult as it is to translate the general vocabulary, it is still more difficult to translate Hebrew terms designating the mores of Jewish life. Thus the word *mitzvah*, literally trans- lated as commandment, conveys in its Hebrew usage also many other associations, such as religious duty, or a good deed, or a function in a synagogue service. *Bar Mitzvah*, literally, "a son of commandment" is, as we have seen, the designation given to a lad when he becomes thirteen years of age. The term proclaims him to be henceforth personally re- sponsible for carrying out the behests of Jewish religious life. To translate Bar Mitzvah by confirmation as is not infre- quently done gives an altogether misleading character to the term. Confirmation suggests a formal adherence to confirmed belief in dogma and doctrine, whereas the Hebrew term Bar Mitzvah implies the assumption of religious duties by action and conduct. A Bar Mitzvah boy is asked not for a confirma- tion in dogma but for acceptance of the practises of Jewish religious life.

We cannot expect to find the connotations of the Hebrew word *Shabbat* in the transliterated word Sabbath. The very fact that there could grow up such a phrase as "the witches' Sabbath" shows that the Hebraic conception of the Sabbath day of rest, release and inspiration, has not been fully trans- mitted in its counterpart. To translate *Yom tov*, the designa- tion of days such as the Passover, Pentecost and Tabernacles, as festival or holiday secularizes it. It fails to evoke the religious ceremonial, the synagogue ritual, the domestic felicity, song, and traditional meals, all part of a unique

complex of joy and sanctification implicit in the phrase
Yom tov.

It would require a small volume to convey all the unique
associations of the Hebrew word *kasher* or *kosher*. It is a
term applied to permitted foods. An aura of fidelity and
purity has surrounded the ritual of kosher food since Bible
days, and has given that word its unique overtones and
associations. Its virtual untranslatability has brought about its
growing recognition in the English language, and it is now
to be found in modern English dictionaries.

The Book of Proverbs (18:2) expresses a profound truth
in its statement that "death and life are in the power of the
tongue." One of the reasons why the important Greek-speak-
ing Jewry of Alexandria of olden days died out was because
they forgot their Hebrew. On the other hand, it is strangely
moving to find that a password among the Marranos, the
secret Jews who attempted to escape persecution by the
Spanish Inquisition, was the inviolately preserved Hebrew
name for the Lord. This one Hebrew word which they held
in common with free Jews led to the final dramatic recognition of this Jewish remnant which had survived five centuries of duress.

Hebrew has been so much a reality throughout Jewish
history that under the influence of the single-minded individual Eleazar Ben Jehudah, Zionists returning to the ancestral Promised Land were able to adapt the classic *leshon
hakodesh,* "sacred tongue," for use as the modern language
of Israel. The Hebrew language is a unifying force among
the immigrants to that land who have come bringing
with them a Babel of mother tongues from innumerable
countries, to mention only Russia, Roumania, Hungary,
Germany, Italy, Holland, England, Latin America, India,
Bokhara, Iraq, and Iran. Hebrew was the common language
that they could make their own with its unique and unifying

Jewish associations. They all say *shalom*, "peace," as the traditional greeting. In Hebrew that word means all that peace means, but it also carries with it etymological and literary associations of wholeness, wellbeing, good health, prosperity, harmony, soundness and the absence of factors disturbing spiritual and physical welfare. In that one word of greeting the Jew of today is linked with the earliest Bible times as far back as the day when Jacob approaching the home of Laban asked as to Laban's *shalom*.

The Hebrew language is an essential of Judaism and of Jewish life. It associates the individual Jew with the Bible and the synagogue, with the religious conscience of the Jewish people, with the millennial span of Jewish history and literature, and in our day also with the third Jewish commonwealth in Israel with its Hebrew renascent.

So long as a people's language lives that people's distinctive spirit can live. Hebrew has never been allowed to become a dead language. In all the nineteen centuries and in all the five continents of the dispersion of the Jewish people since the destruction of their homeland by the Romans, the Hebrew language has lived on. It is beautifully true that man has been blessed by the Bible of the Jew in whatever language it has been translated. But its original Hebrew text remains the supreme instrument for expressing its transcendence. Happy is the Jew who can call the Hebrew language and the Hebrew Bible his own.

TWELVE

EVENTFUL DAYS

ONE sometimes wonders why the Jew has been happy in his Judaism seeing how demanding are its observances and how beset with suffering his life has been. One answer is that the Jewish child in his earliest and most impressionable years has seen the distinctive poetry, beauty and spiritual uplift of Judaism transforming what else might easily be a drab order of living. Some nineteen centuries ago Philo of Alexandria trenchantly said that there are ten festivals in the Jewish calendar and the first of these is every day. The forms and ceremonies of Judaism put into daily life infinite possibilities of beauty and spiritual inspiration. One needs but mention the recurrent seventh day Sabbath the growing anticipation of which traditionally colors all the six working days of the week. In addition, the beginning of each new month is anticipated by special prayers in the synagogue, and the opening of each month, Rosh Hodesh, is in itself a minor religious festival.

The Jewish New Year's Day, Rosh Hashanah, occurs in the early fall. It is a unique combination of rejoicing and solemnity. On the one hand it recalls Nehemiah's proclama

tion (8:10) to the Jews of Jerusalem, "This day is holy to the
Lord your God, mourn not nor weep . . . Go, eat rich
dainties and drink sweet drinks, and send portions to him
who has nothing ready, for this day is holy to our Lord.
Grieve not, for the joy of the Lord is your strength." At
the same time, the New Year's Day celebration has never been
an excuse for unrestrained merrymaking. It is also characterized by solemn anticipation and as a moral and religious
preparation for the year to come.

To rise from workaday interests to soul-searching cannot
be effected by push-button automation. Nor can one lightly
penetrate from material superficialities to the depths of the
human soul. To pass from one to the other, the Jew builds
a bridge of preparedness with the coming of the New Year.
The foundations are laid during the preceding days by
special prayers of confessional devotion, self-examination,
and supplication for forgiveness attuning the spirit for the
oncoming New Year's Day. It is a day conceived of as the
awesome time when the record of man's works is reviewed in
judgment. The Book of Life is opened in the heavenly court
on that day, and from every heart rises the yearning to be
found worthy of his name being inscribed in the Book of
Life in the new year which is dawning. Following the Biblical regulation, the clamant ram's horn, the *shofar*, is sternly
sounded as a summons to judgment. Did not the prophet
Amos (3:6), say "Shall a horn be blown in the city and the
people be not afraid?"

Rosh Hashanah, New Year's Day, ushers in ten days of
penitence. They are a preparation for the concentrated fervor
of the Day of Atonement, Yom Kippur, the day supremely
and wholly dedicated to confession and self-purification. The
Mishnah emphasizes that a wrong done to a fellow man
cannot be expiated on Yom Kippur without the wrong being
righted. The Ten Days of Penitence call for reconciling one

who has been hurt, and making any needed restitution. Only then, after one has done all that is in his power to right his relations with his fellow men, may he on the Day of Atonement seek reconciliation with his Maker.

"Kol Nidre" has become a familiar phrase since its moving ancient melody was set to modern musical notation by Max Bruch. To that chant a declaration is thrice recited on the eve of the Day of Atonement immediately preceding the opening service. The scrolls of the Torah are brought to the reading desk of the synagogue to invest the moment with the greatest solemnity. The rabbi or the hazzan then intones the formula of the Kol Nidre. It is one which absolves any who in the preceding year may have failed in a vow between themselves and their Maker. This formula of absolution came to birth in the early Middle Ages for Jews who had been given the alternative of death or abjuration of their faith. On this night of nights some of these would covertly find their way back to their people and to the worship which under duress they had been compelled outwardly to renounce. Then with intense emotion the rabbi declared null and void the vows of apostasy cruelly wrung from them, and formally permitted these unhappy brothers, transgressors against Judaism though they were, to rejoin their people in penitential prayer. During the ages this Kol Nidre formula of absolution became broadened to apply to all vows between oneself and one's Creator. It never did, and it does not, for it cannot, release anyone from any juridical oath, or from any promise, vow, contract, or obligation between man and man.

On the Day of Atonement Jews give themselves to spiritual exercise that makes physical concession only to the need of sleep at night. Abstention from food and drink on this day symbolizes the rejection of all materialities and the dedication to inner contemplation and at-one-ment with the Infinite. Freed from the trammels of the flesh, from mundane exigencies and distractions, and from disturbing trivialities of the daily routine, the Jew takes refuge within the sanctuary of his faith. On this day he lives altogether on the plane of the eternal soul. He gives himself to fearless introspection and asking the Divine within him and above him to help him correct the flaws in the texture of his living. He lays on the altar his spiritual offering of remorse for failures in the past and his determination to achieve amendment in the future. In days of yore the elder would address the congregation saying, "Brethren, our Bible tells us concerning the people of Nineveh not that God saw their sackcloth and their fasting, but that He saw their actions that they had turned from their evil way" (Jonah 3:10).

Underlying Yom Kippur's solemn consciousness of sin is a philosophy of invincible optimism, a firm belief in the forgiveness which follows true penitence, and a wholesome conviction that man by his own ability can attain virtue. The Jew believes profoundly in the possibilities of purity of the human soul. He rejects the teaching which depicts the soul as held in the grip of sin, and he repudiates a way of life which tends to a continued self-flagellation and a morbid ingrowing sense of sin. He can thus face life with an inspiriting sense of innate human worth even during the days devoted to searching penitential introspection. This is the message which the Day of Atonement brings to him, that the God of justice and retribution is also the God of understanding, forgiveness and lovingkindness. Repeated with the impact of a crescendo throughout the day is the revelation to Moses of God's nature and attributes: "The Lord, the Lord, God compassionate and gracious, long-suffering and abundant in mercy and truth, keeping mercy for thousands, forgiving iniquity, transgression and sin, and absolving" (Exodus 34:6).

During the whole of the day he seeks to live in the spirit of the Psalmist who with a broken and a contrite heart prayed for the creation of a clean heart and the renewal of a right spirit within him (51:12, 19). He seeks with the prophet of old (Isaiah 58:6) to make a reality of the day of fasting by "loosening the fetters of wickedness, undoing the bonds of the yoke, sending the oppressed free and breaking every yoke." He believes that no priest can shrive and absolve anyone from his sin, and no angelic interceder, no mediating savior, no beatified pleader, can come between the individual's soul and his God. The obligation rests inescapably on each to cleanse his own soul through communing and finding the right way of life by inward struggle.

There is but one Day of Atonement, but there are other days which have been designated for fasting because of their associations with the destruction of the first Temple. The prophet Zechariah mentions (8:19) "the fast of the fourth month, and the fast of the fifth month, and the fast of the seventh month, and the fast of the tenth month." The fast of the fifth month falling on the ninth day of the month of Ab is the major one of these minor fast days. It still commands the deepest emotional recognition. In cumulative coincidences, the ninth day of the month of Ab is associated with a long succession of tragic events. It is primarily the anniversary of the destruction of both King Solomon's Temple and the post-Biblical Herodian Temple in Jerusalem. But also on that day, the ninth of Ab, in 1571 the city of Florence instituted the ghetto, as on that day Rome had done sixteen years earlier. In 1492 on the ninth of Ab, as Columbus was about to set sail on the morrow on his world-opening voyage of discovery, inquisitorial Spain ordered the banishment of her Jews. On that day, the ninth of the month of Ab, in 1290 there was signed the decree of expulsion of Jews from England. On that day in the year 135 the struggle of Judea for regaining its independence was bloodily crushed by Roman legions. On that day in the

following year 136 the plough was driven over the ground
which had been the Holy City. On that day sixty-five years
earlier, Jerusalem with its Temple and the Jewish state were
destroyed by the Romans, as on that day six and a half
centuries earlier Jerusalem with its Temple and the Jewish
state had been destroyed by the Babylonians. On that day of
iterative tragic memories, the ninth day of the month
of Ab, evening and morning, Jews, fasting, have gathered in
darkened synagogues, taken off their formal leather shoes,
sat on the ground in mourning, and chanted the Lamentations of Jeremiah, dirges and other plaintive songs of woe.
But in the afternoon the congregation rises up to chant prophetic words of comfort and undying hope—"Comfort ye
comfort ye My people, says your God" (Isaiah 40:1).

This note of solace remains. The memories which color
Jewish observance are not predominantly sad. They are for
the most part happy and bright, and over and over again they
hark back to the land of the Bible and its agricultural civilization. Thus on the fifteenth day of the Hebrew month of She-
bat, the New Year for Trees, penitential prayers are omitted
from the liturgy. Though it is still winter in northern climes,
the Jew then partakes of figs, dates, and other fruits that
grow in the Promised Land, because at that time the sap
rises in its trees, portending the advent of spring and summer
fruitfulness. Winter's hard protective scales on the trees now
will begin to burst, and the buds will break forth to new
life. Whether herded within the dark and treeless narrow
stony lanes of the ghettos, or in snow-covered towns, or in
tropical heat, the Jew kept before him a joyous vision of
flowers and trees, fruits and harvests, in his ancestral home.

The three dominant festival periods in the Jewish calendar,
Passover (*Pesah*), Pentecost (*Shabuoth*), and Tabernacles
(*Sukkoth*), celebrate important turning points in the agricul-
tural cycle of the Holy Land. Symbolically they are occasions

of thanksgiving and blessing for the life-giving food brought forth from all the earth. Passover marks the springtime of hope and the harvesting of the early ripening barley. "For lo, the winter is past, the rain is over and gone, flowers bedeck the earth . . . the fig tree ripeneth her green fruits, the blossoming vines give forth their fragrance" (Song of Songs 2:11–13). On Passover the world over the idyl of the Biblical Song of Songs is read, and prayers are offered in synagogues for copious fructifying dews in the fields of the Holy Land during the approaching rainless summer.

Thereafter, for seven weeks the Jew daily recalls that on the Passover there was brought the first offering of a sheaf from the early barley harvest. "You shall count for yourselves from the morrow after the (Passover) day of rest, from the day of your bringing the sheaf (*Omer*) of the wave-offering; seven weeks shall there be complete, until the morrow of the seventh week you shall count fifty days" (Leviticus 23: 15, 16). At the close of those fifty ("Pentecost") days of counting occurs Shabuoth, "Weeks," the harvest festival of the first-fruits and later ripening grains. It is then customary to bedeck the synagogue and the home with greenery and flowers of the field. The idyl of the Book of Ruth is read on Shabuoth, and even under the most urban conditions one follows the gentle Ruth's gleaning in the fields of Boaz. The Torah especially enjoins that at all the three harvest festivals every-one gathering in his crop shall allow the poor to share in his personal harvest, a usage touchingly described in Ruth's free gleaning in the fields of Boaz.

The third harvest festival, Tabernacles (Sukkoth "Booths"), occurring as the summer mellows into autumn, celebrates the thanksgiving for the ripened fruit of the final harvest. The American holiday of Thanksgiving Day has developed from the early Bible-loving settlers having adopted the Biblical Tabernacles festival of thanksgiving. Since George Washington's first presidential call for a national Thanksgiving Day on November 26, 1789, and even from a third of a century earlier, my Congregation Shearith Israel in keeping with its loyalty to both its Jewish and its American heritage has celebrated Thanksgiving Day.

During the week of Sukkoth, the Jew sings glad hymns of praise and thanksgiving as he waves his *lulab* (palm branch) cluster, a palm branch held in the hand together with branches of myrtle and willow, and a citron. He is also called on to erect a *sukkah*. This is a temporary dwelling modelled after the harvest booth of the fields. Its roof is a frail covering made up of branches of trees loosely laid across the top so that the stars may be seen through it at night. Its walls are customarily decorated with fruit, such as clusters of grapes, pomegranates, gourds, pictures and ornaments, recalling Israel's harvesting. The sukkah is a center of rejoicing and open house hospitality and sociability. The three harvest festivals, Passover, Pentecost, and Tabernacles, revive each in its turn the Biblical command (Deuteronomy 16:14), "You shall rejoice in your festival, you and your son, and your daughter, and your manservant and your maidservant, and the Levite, and the stranger, and the orphan, and the widow who are within your gates." The medieval Jewish philosopher Maimonides declared that to rejoice around the table in one's home or sukkah with the family but without some of the poor and the homeless sharing in the festival's happiness and bounty may satisfy the individual self; but it does not express the cheer and gladness with which we are enjoined to celebrate our religious festivals. The poor guest at the table, said one of the rabbis, gives more to his host than the host can give to him. Charity blesses the giver even more than the receiver.

The fall harvest does not spell the end of the agricultural cycle in the land of the Bible. The summer dryness should be followed by the "former rain." Those autumnal rains together with the "latter rain" of late winter would bring the promise of life itself to the land and its people. If the expected rain were scanty or were to fail, crops might wither, wells and streams run dry, and stark want or even famine might loom for man and beast. Therefore on Tabernacles there were daily circuits around the altar in the Jerusalem Temple while there rose up the supplication *Hosanna* "O save us." Then there was offered up devout prayer that rain would fall in its due season with mercy for mankind. On the seventh day, *Hoshaana Rabbah*, "the Great Hosanna, the great prayer 'O save us,'" seven such circuits were made around the altar. The Jewish consciousness has vividly preserved the realization of how great is the blessing when there is fulfilled God's word (Deuteronomy 11:14, 15), "I will send the rain for your land in its due season, the autumn rain and the spring rain, that you may gather in your corn, your wine, and your oil, and I will give grass in your field for your cattle, and you shall eat and be satisfied." Some Jews realize the essential nature of this blessing so strongly that on the eve of Hoshaana Rabbah they spend the whole night reading religious writings in mystic preparation for the morning service with its seven circuits, so that they may be the more worthy on this day of the Great Hosanna. A fervent prayer for rain is offered up in synagogues everywhere on the eighth day of the festival of Tabernacles. This steadfast and persistent clinging to the ancient agricultural associations of life in the Holy Land moved Disraeli prophetically to say a century ago that "a race that persist in celebrating their vintage, although they have no fruit to gather, will regain their vineyards."

The message of these festivals is enriched by memories of cardinal moments in Jewish history, each of which has also been deeply significant for mankind.

Passover (Pesah), the spring festival of new life from the soil, is also the festival of the renewed life which came to the children of Israel with their triumphant exodus from the oppressive land of Egypt three thousand two hundred years ago. Its theme is redemption from bondage, tyranny and suffering. The emancipation of the Jewish people presaged the birth of freedom among men. The Passover story is the oldest Declaration of Independence that mankind knows. It gives an inspiring vision of national life founded on liberty under God and law.

The Jew is seldom happier than on the eve of the Passover. Preceding it there has been the busy search for leaven in every corner of the home, in keeping with the Biblical ordinance to remove all leaven. Dishes have been changed, and special symbolic foods have been prepared, particularly unleavened bread, matzah, and a hors d'oeuvre of bitter herbs. Finally, in joyous expectation there gather around the festive table the family and many friends. It is the time the Bible calls "the night of vigilance" (Exodus 12:42). Then with vivid question and answer and much song the Biblical injunction is fulfilled that every year on the Passover there shall be retold the story of the birth of freedom for the children of Israel. In retelling that story of the freeing of his ancestors, every Jew relives it personally. For he recalls the Biblical comment on the eating of unleavened bread during the week of Passover (Exodus 13:8): "You shall tell your son on that day, saying, it is because of what the Lord did for *me* when I came out of Egypt." These words are interpreted by the rabbis as intimating that everyone should regard himself as if he personally had come forth from Egypt. In this flight of imagination, the Passover Haggadah, "recital," of a vicarious experience three thousand years old dowers the children in each generation with a renewed love of liberty.

From the suffering and forced labor which the children of

Israel endured under Pharaoh they found their way to freedom under law. A horde of slaves became a nation. The message of Passover is a protest against oppression and the denial of human liberty, the call to faith that freedom will ultimately triumph, and that man must and will be redeemed from tyrannous dictatorship, cruelty, and oppression.

In every generation the lessons of Moses have been translated into terms relevant to contemporary social and political problems. Thus the Passover today rings out a protest against fascism, communism, and the Pharaohs of our times. Its basic call for freedom is echoed in every good fight against injustice and discrimination exercised against any racial or religious group. It is a potent protest against religious bigotry, race prejudice, class prejudice, and racial and social segregation. It is a reverberating protest against any infringement of personal freedom and freedom of conscience. It gives the Jew a deepened appreciation of the privilege of being a Jew.

Seven weeks after Passover comes the festival of Shabuoth, "Pentecost." In those seven weeks of the Omer, as we have seen, every day is counted in looking forward to the Shabuoth festival of the first-fruits. They have become weeks during which the historic memories of the Jew also bid him count the days in a less happy spirit. For those bright spring days have all too often been darkened by sorrow and suffering, so much so that the custom has spread of not celebrating a marriage or indulging in other festivities during a considerable period of the seven weeks.

Then at their close comes the Feast of Weeks, Shabuoth. On that day the divine revelation of the Ten Commandments was given to the children of Israel. These brought to man the freedom which meant even more than the absence of the taskmaster. The Torah offered emancipation from superstition, from idolatry, and from social evils, through the freedom by which man can live to his utmost potential, freedom under law. Shabuoth, the celebration of the harvesting of the first-fruits of the cultivation of the soil is also the celebration of the harvesting of the first-fruits of the cultivation of the soul.

Tabernacles (Sukkoth) recalls the forty disciplinary years of desert wandering. These were a training for freedom under law. The children of Israel were bidden never to forget that soul-testing experience. They were enjoined to dwell in frail booths *"sukkoth"* during the weeks of Tabernacles, "so that your generations may know that I made the children of Israel dwell in booths when I brought them out of the land of Egypt" (Leviticus 23:43).

Tabernacles is immediately followed by the unique *Simhath Torah*, "the Rejoicing in the Torah." This is the festival of the Book. Scrolls of the Torah are carried around the synagogue in gay processions with gladsome song. Children are especially singled out for attention. They are given goodies and are encouraged to march in the circuits. At the morning service the annual consecutive reading of the whole Torah comes to a close with the final chapters of Deuteronomy. But finis can never be said of the Torah, and this reading is immediately followed by the opening chapter of Genesis. There is no hiatus, no ending, and once more the reading of the Pentateuch goes on anew from the beginning. There is no interruption in the unending cycle.

Joyous also is the carnival folk festival of Purim. The Book of Esther (9:22) records that on that day "the Jews got relief from their enemies, and the month that had been turned for them from sorrow to gladness and from mourning to a holiday, that they should make them days of feasting and gladness, and sending portions to one another and gifts to the poor." Purim is exuberantly celebrated with masques, parody and gibe, and the clean wholesome laughter to which healthy recognition is given in Jewish religious life. It is truly remarkable that the centuries of bitter prejudice and persecution to which the Jew has been subjected failed to create in him a persecution complex. Haman, ruthless persecutor though he was, is portrayed as a stupid buffoon who is mocked and burlesqued with uproarious laughter in convivial celebration. This is a very real demonstration of the absence of vindictiveness that characterizes Jewish memories of the Hamans of history.

One other festival, Hanukkah, "Dedication," like Passover and Purim, also celebrates the miracle of Jewish survival. It recalls how twenty-one hundred years ago the Jewish people led by the military genius of Judas Maccabeus regained its independence. Through heroic resistance against the demented Antiochus Epiphanes, who pathologically sought to impose in terms of his day what we call totalitarian tyranny, the Maccabean revolt vindicated the right of freedom of conscience, and rescued Judaism from being engulfed by paganism. The few overcame the many, and the unarmed triumphed over powerful warriors. They asserted the strength of spiritual power over physical violence. The Maccabees in their day destroyed a Gestapo of organized terror over men's minds and souls. So far-reaching was the importance of this victory, the story of which is told in the Apocrypha, that the observance of Hanukkah has always been regarded by the Jew as no less authoritatively called for than that of the festivals prescribed by the Bible. Hanukkah marks the fulfilment of the vision that "the people who walked in darkness have seen a great light" (Isaiah 9.1). Each evening for eight days lights are progressively kindled in the home, one on the first night, two on the second, and so on. These lights are put in the window or the doorway so that others may share in the undying faith in the ever-growing triumph of spiritual light over physical might. The Hanukkah lights express the Jew's indomitable faith that the light of liberty and religious

freedom which he kept alive in many dark ages shall yet shine
forth unquenchably for all.

This bird's-eye view of the memorable days in the Jewish
calendar may well recall a remark made by the rabbis in the
time of the Roman Empire when they looked out on the
pagan holidays with their Bacchanals of immoderate eating,
excessive drinking, and frenzied flocking to the arena heart-
lessly to watch lions and gladiators maul or kill one another.
They commented on the contrast with the holidays in Jewish
life when there was eating and drinking with moderation
while thanking God for the blessing of the food and drink,
and instead of thronging to the amphitheatre there was
gathering in synagogues to sing joyful praises of God. What
these rabbis noted of the spirit of Jewish holidays two thousand years ago has not changed.

To this day a Jewish life makes a glad renewal of every day,
and not only of an occasional festival or holy day. At all
times it helps one evaluate the speeding of time. Every morning in the year the Jew blesses God who revives each day
His work of creation. Workaday, Sabbath, festival, holiday,
and holy day, each brings its meed to the creation of meaningful living, and helps explain why I am glad I am a Jew.

THIRTEEN

IS JUDAISM LEGALISTIC?

THROUGH the windows of holy days and holidays we have perhaps caught some glimpse of what it means to be a Jew. The most important words in the Bible, the rabbis state, are (Proverbs 3:6): "In all your ways know Him and He will direct your paths." Not only on special occasions but every day in the year Judaism can be penetratingly felt. It comes to expression in innumerable ways in ceremonial and ritual observances.

All too often it is assumed that the religious spirit in Judaism is overweighted by these forms. Those who have not experienced the uplift of its ceremonies may be inclined to believe that in Judaism the letter of the law destroys its spirit. The brief summary which has been given here of the traditional Jewish observances shows how ceremonial can give reality to such abstract concepts as atonement, liberty, law, thanksgiving, and *joie de vivre*. These have been clothed by a people's psyche in historically conditioned and readily transmissible ceremonial. The concept of atonement is made a vivid actuality by the fasting and ritual of Yom Kippur. Do we wish to celebrate and make real the idea of liberty? It is not left to each individual to choose his own forms and formulas for doing this. History and Biblical regulations have created in the Passover a unifying ceremonial which not only expresses for the whole people a religious appreciation of human freedom, but also engenders and by repetition strengthens and ingrains it. We cannot belittle the association of freedom with unleavened bread any more than we can rationalize away the association of patriotism with a colored cloth we call a flag. Such historical associations have the binding sanctity which comes to them from accrued sentiment over long generations. Similarly the majesty of law, the felicity of thanksgiving, and the sunshine of happy living are dramatized so that all can feel them by the festival celebration of Pentecost, Tabernacles and Purim.

The vividness of response to this ceremonial will vary with individual sensitiveness, measure of religious hunger, emotional background, atmosphere in the home, childhood associations, early training, personal experiences, and knowledge of Judaism, of Hebrew language and literature and of Jewish history. Experience over millennia has shown that the influence of ceremonial and ritual is cumulative. What preparation they require adds to the receptivity of the faithful. What sacrifice their observance may call for but enhances their meaning.

Difficulty, however, has not of itself been made a virtue by the Bible and by the rabbis who formulated the observances of Judaism. Moses affirmed (Deuteronomy 30:10–13) to the children of Israel that the injunction which he was giving them to keep the commandments written in the Torah was not too onerous for them, nor was it remote. "It is not in heaven so that you should say, 'Who will go up for us to heaven and bring it to us that we may hear it and do it.' Nor is it beyond the sea that you should say, 'Who will go over the sea for us and bring it to us so that we may hear it and do it.' But the word is very near to you, in your mouth and in your heart so that you can do it."

Authoritative Jewish tradition consistently discountenances asceticism, self-castigation, mortification of the spirit, penances, excessive fasting, world abnegation and other austerities. Nevertheless, religion demands effort. An easy discipline is no discipline. The popular phrase "easy virtue" shows how an easy morality can come perilously close to being no morality.

Through its legalism and ceremonial, Judaism endows physical acts with symbolic meaning and links personal observance with the unbroken chain of history. It brings uplift to the routine of living. It makes even the commonplace an instrument of inner communion. For me, Jewish legalism has united matter and mind, body and soul, in a synthesis of transcendant harmony.

In summing up his questionings as to the meaning and purpose of life Ecclesiastes declared (12:13) this is "the end of the matter, all has been heard revere God and keep His commandments; for this is the whole duty of man." The rabbis had a keen awareness of the fundamental simplicity and unity of the moral law alongside the manifold complexities of conduct and social relations.

One of them counted no less than six hundred and thirteen commandments in the Five Books of Moses. But Rabbi Simlai said that David in the fifteenth Psalm reduced them to eleven, Isaiah (33:15) reduced them to six—walk righteously, speak uprightly, despise gain from oppression, refuse to take a bribe, close one's ears against bloodshed, refuse to look on evil, Micah (6:8) to three—"to do justly, to love mercy, and to walk humbly with God," Isaiah (56:1) again to two—"keep justice and do righteousness," Amos (5:4) to one—"seek Me and live," and Habakkuk (2:4) also to one, "the righteous shall live by his faithfulness." Rabbi Akiba saw in the Biblical command

(Leviticus 19:18) "You shall love your neighbor as yourself" the farthest reaching summation of religious duty.

We all know that man cannot breathe pure oxygen or maintain his physical health by eating only the essential chemical quintessence of bulky food. A religion of abstractions faces the danger of losing its hold on reality. We are not living in a world of disembodied spirits. However emotionally we may extol charity, until we actually practise it, it remains unreal. Man's spirit cannot come to full emotional expression when nourished only by formulas. It needs a body of religious forms to give permeating and transmissible expression to the concentrate of pure ethical thought. Judaism holds that virtue is most readily attained through the practise of virtues. Reverence in prayer is furthered by such physical actions as closing the eyes or bowing. A sense of holiness is made more realistic by such a purely physical procedure as reverent washing the hands before entering a synagogue. When emotion leaves us distraught as in the hour of mourning, traditional practises such as reciting through one's tears the ordained prayers for the dead help assuage sorrow and strengthen the heart. Moses Maimonides pointedly affirmed that the general object of the Torah is twofold, the well-being of the soul and that of the body. Its laws create a comprehensive way of life and bring to transcendant expression its high purposes.

Because their intent is healthy normal living, all the rules, regulations and traditional observances of Judaism cede their primacy to helping the sick or saving the endangered. A doctor may order his patient to eat on a fast day. In serving the sick the physician may work on the Sabbath. The rabbis clearly enunciated the principle that the Sabbath was instituted for Israel, not Israel for the Sabbath. When the Roman emperor Hadrian imposed the death penalty for Jewish observances, the rabbis ruled that one might disregard every commandment excepting only three from which no exemption could be permitted. These were the prohibition of idolatry, of murder, and of adultery. In the beginning of the Maccabean war waged to regain freedom for the Jewish people and their religion, many were cut down in cold blood because they would not take up arms on the Sabbath. The ruling was then made that in the life and death emergency of war the Sabbath laws are not binding. Had not Amos been told by God (5:4) "Seek Me and *live*"? Did not the prophet Habakkuk say (2:4), "The righteous shall *live* by his faithfulness"?

When evaluating the relation between observance and principle, between letter and spirit, it should be remembered that the word "religion" is derived from the Latin word "religio" which comes to mean a faithful and vigilant observance of rules. It is the opposite of "negligio." In this spirit, Jewish legalism regulates and gives an aura of sanctity to every act of life. The hundred blessings a day which the tradition entails are specifically for all experiences: for the foodstuffs which we eat in nature's abundant variety; for the sweet odors of herbs, flowers, spices and perfumes; for sounds that we hear, whether they may spell good tidings or bad tidings; for awe-inspiring, beautiful, or strange sights, a rainbow, lightning, mountains, the ocean, beautiful trees, the glorious phenomena of nature, or men distinguished by position or wisdom; for the sense of touch such as in the wearing of new clothes, and indeed for the most varied experiences of sheer physical living. We can all help fulfil the injunction given through Joshua (1:8), "This book of the Torah shall not depart out of your mouth, but you shall meditate on it day and night." We can all emulate the Psalmist who said (16:8), "I keep the Lord before me at all times."

It is significant that these words of the Psalmist are the

opening and the keynote of the Shulhan Arukh, the sum-
marized code with its myriad regulations which give distinctive character to the life of the Jew. The true effect of Jewish
legalism is to bring man into continuous fellowship with
God. Judaism is not an abstraction to be distantly pondered;
it is a reality which suffuses every aspect of daily living. It
is an ever-present staff on which one may safely lean. To
wait for the unaided spirit to move, may mean for many to
wait long or in vain. Religious expression would be indeed
sporadic and fitful if left to fortuitous individual impulse.
Therefore with keen psychological insight Judaism institutes
set times and occasions for rites which help engender and
stimulate religious feeling and bring it to expression.

There is of course the danger that some will substitute
the letter for the spirit. Religious rites may become perfunc-
tory and formalistic. But greater is the opposite danger that an
antinomian disdain of ceremonial and ritual may lead to a
loss of religion. In Judaism the spirit has not been destroyed
by the letter. It is the Levitical law, a classic instance of
legalism, which in the midst of detailed minutiae of observance proclaims (19:18), "You shall love your neighbor as
yourself." Ezekiel, among the prophets the ritualist par excellence, is also the prophet of the heart. The Temple of old,
the home of the ritual of sacrifice, produced as its hymn book
the Book of Psalms, the supremely spiritual outcry of man to
God. Joseph Caro, the compiler of the Shulhan Arukh, the
code of Jewish legalism spoken of above, was a profound
mystic. No Jewish observance is subject to more regulations
than is the Sabbath, and hundreds of rulings define what
is considered to be work and therefore an encroachment on
Sabbath rest. Yet there is no more spiritual experience than
the Sabbath with its mystic inwardness, its warmth and its
domestic loveliness, all evoked by the very regimen set up

by the Sabbath laws. These laws expressive of religion are felt to be not restrictions but creatively stimulating.

This organized institution of observances also makes Judaism transmissible as the religion of a whole people. It discourages the growth of variegated sectarianism. It unifies Jewry and preserves Jewish identity. It places the obligations of Judaism on all alike. It has helped ensure organic continuity, and has created spatial as well as temporal unity in Jewish life for over three thousand years. It is the legalism of the Torah which in all the past generations has maintained the Jewish people as a coherent, organic, integrated whole. It is the letter of the law which has preserved the spirit and endowed it with the strength to grow and recreate itself ever anew.

FOURTEEN

THE JEWISH HOME

THE STRONGEST formative Jewish influence, continous and permeating, has been that of the home. It is central to many religious ceremonies such as the Sabbath, the Passover eve gathering around the table to recount the birth of freedom, the week of thanksgiving spent in the harvest booth at Tabernacles, the lighting of the candles at Hanukkah, or the convivial gatherings which characterize Purim. A Jewish home colored by historical tradition is pervaded by such influences not occasionally but day and night from the outward doorpost to its inmost privacy. It is a place in which one lives, not a retreat to which one comes to sleep.

It is in the home that the influence of women is most strongly exercised. In Biblical days the Jewish woman took her part alongside of man in many activities. One need but mention Miriam or Deborah to illustrate this. Women also took an active part in religious activities. To give but a few examples: of Rebecca we are told (Genesis 25:23) that she went to inquire of the Lord, just as Hannah journeyed to the tabernacle in Shiloh in fulfilment of her religious obligations (I Samuel 1, 2). A woman, Huldah, is mentioned as a prophetess (II Kings 22:14). The final words of Moses (Deuteronomy 29:9, 10) are addressed to those assembled, who were all the men of Israel with their wives and little ones. It is true, as has been mentioned, that in the development of Jewish practise women were excused from a number of ritual obligations which had to be carried out at a set time; but in this there was no derogation of the respect paid to them. The opinions of Beruriah, the wife of Rabbi Meir, are quoted by the rabbis with high approval. Ben Azzai, one of the leading rabbis of his day, stated that a man must teach Torah to his daughter. In general the rabbis declared that the Holy One, blessed be He, gave to women an understanding surpassing that of men.

It is marriage not celibacy, which expresses the Jewish ideal of fulfilled living. Over and over again the prophets of the Bible figuratively speak of the people of Israel as united in marriage with their God in a covenant of love. Judaism holds that marriages are made in heaven. When one of the rabbis was asked by a Roman matron what his God had been doing since He completed the work of creation, the answer was that He had been making marriages. Indeed, a popular Talmudic saying declares that forty days before the birth of a boy a heavenly voice proclaims that the daughter of so and so will be destined to become his wife.

The world over, pietists, both men and women, in their quest of purity have often regarded marriage as an evil that may deflect them from spiritual living. In sharp contrast, traditional Jewish teaching regards being unmarried as a hindrance to and an impoverishment of one's spiritual life. Marriage is looked on as a religious duty and sacrament. One of the rabbis said that he did not refer to his wife as wife but as home. The very beginning of the Biblical word declares (Genesis 2:18) that "it is not good that man should be alone." The urge of sex is not just an animal instinct;

it is also a sublimated potent driving force which leads man
to build a home and establish a family. One rabbi went so far
as to say that he who has no wife is not worthy of the name
of man. Another declared that such a man lives without
happiness, without blessing, and without good. In this spirit
Ecclesiastes (9:9) urged "enjoy life with the wife whom you
love," and the Book of Proverbs said (18:22, 12:4, 19:14)
that "he who finds a wife has found a great good," for "a
virtuous wife is the crown of her husband," "an understanding wife is from the Lord." The rabbis indeed require a man
to give greater consideration to his wife and children than to
himself. Since the time of Rabbenu Gershom in the tenth
century a man is not permitted to divorce his wife without
her consent.

"Be fruitful and multiply" is the first commandment given
in the Bible (Genesis 1:22). A father of children is considered
as through them continuing his life beyond death. The
rabbis urge that a man should marry at not later than
eighteen years of age in order to safeguard his morality, fulfil his own personality, and facilitate the establishment of a
family. The section of the Jewish code which deals with
marriage opens with the incisive statement that he who remains unmarried is as it were one who sheds blood. He
diminishes the likeness of God among mankind, for man is
created in the image of God. In Hebrew the term used for
marriage is *kiddushin*, that is, sanctification, hallowing. The
rabbis declare that among the first questions asked of a man
on the day of judgment are "did you marry?" and "have you
founded a family?" Children are indeed what the Psalmist
(127:3) calls "a heritage of the Lord."

The sanctity, happiness, and integrity traditionally and
rightly associated with the Jewish home owe much to the
Biblical laws of purity and sex. They are basic to the love of
husband and wife and children which has made the Jewish

home one of uncommon beauty. The rabbis said to one who loves his wife as himself and honors her more than he honors himself, who brings up his sons and daughters in the right paths and who sees that they marry while yet young, "you will know that your tent is at peace" (Job 5:24). From of old the happy integrity of the family and the Jewish home stood out. It is striking that when the infant Moses, who became the leader of the Jewish people, was compelled to be cast out of his home, he was yet suckled by his own mother, in contrast with Romulus and Remus, legendary founders of the Romans, who when cast out as infants were suckled by a she-wolf. The Negro spiritual "Why Adam was a sinner" penetratingly suggests the answer that he had no "mummie" to train him in what was right and what was wrong.

"Your wife in your inmost home shall be like a fruitful vine, your children around your table shall be as olive plants. Lo, verily, thus shall be blessed the man who reveres the Lord." This is the Psalmist's (128:3, 4) picture of the blessed Jewish home. When the Jerusalem Temple was destroyed by the Romans, two leading rabbis of the day helped comfort their people by declaring that henceforth the table in the home could and should take the place of the altar in the Temple. Eating is made to be something more than a necessary physical function; it is spiritualized into an instrument of religious service. "Man does not live by bread alone" (Deuteronomy 8:3). Therefore the partaking of food is associated with ceremonials of laving and blessings. The hands are washed and blessings are said as a religious ritual before and after the meal. On breaking bread, blessing is pronounced on God who brings forth bread from the earth. The rabbis meaningfully point out that the apparent contradiction between the Biblical words "The earth is the Lord's and the fulness thereof" and "the earth He has given to the children of men" (Psalm 24:1, 115:16) is resolved when man offers a blessing over the food he has been given which comes from the earth. Simple and brief as is the initial blessing, so by contrast the final blessing of some five hundred succinct Hebrew words, which need nearly double that number for translation, is mystic and transcendent in thought. In its very opening it strikes a universal note by stressing that the Divine hand "gives food for all flesh," "and satisfies all living" (Psalm 136:25, 145:16), and God is blessed for providing food for all, and abundant mercies in grace.

The table is subject to other regulations which express religious sentiment, such as hospitality which must characterize the home, the exclusive use of matzoth, unleavened bread, during the Passover week, avoidance of meat on days of tragic Jewish memories, and observance of the Jewish dietary laws. The Jew is not alone in having religious dietary traditions; virtually every people knowingly or unknowingly has them. Buddhists, Brahmins, Moslems, have their own dietary laws, as have Catholics on Fridays and during Lent. Those of the Jew are laid down in the eleventh chapter of the Book of Leviticus. In brief, they permit meat only of animals that both chew the cud and split the hoof, thus excluding among other animals the pig, the camel, and the horse. Of animals living in the water there are permitted only fish which have both fins and scales, thus barring among others all shellfish, such as shrimps, lobsters, crabs, clams, etc. The Bible repeatedly forbids all eating or drinking of blood. If even a spot of blood is found in an egg, that egg may not be eaten. An animal that is to be killed for food is slaughtered with a razor-sharp knife in a way that virtually drains the body of blood, and that brings instant and merciful unconsciousness. This operation is done with the utmost scrupulousness by a Shohet, ritual slaughterer, who is an educated religious functionary.

Additional to their humane and their devotional aspects,

the Jewish dietary laws contain elements which clearly further the safeguarding of man's health. After the animal is
slaughtered the carcass must be carefully examined. Veins
containing blood are removed. If there are found diseased
conditions such as tubercular lungs, the meat may not be
eaten. Following all such preliminaries the meat is soaked
in water for half an hour, salted for one hour, rinsed again
and then finally it is ready for cooking. Broiling over an open
flame may be substituted for the soaking and salting. Milk
and meat products are kept strictly separate.

The explicit and the only motivation given by the Bible
(Leviticus 11:44, 45) for all the dietary laws is that the Jewish
people shall be holy. In the Jewish home these observances
have had a singularly pervasive influence. As a discipline
they establish a procedure of living which strengthens self-
control. They reinforce sobriety in the enjoyment of food
and drink. They help find a healthy mean between extremes
of ascetic repression and intemperate indulgence. Instead of
a self-flagellating discipline of abnegation and frequent fasts,
they set up a permeating regime of happy self-control exercised every day in the year several times in the day. They have
helped make the Jewish home a model of temperance. They
consecrate the process of eating by making it an integral
part of religion, sublimating the physical into the spiritual.

The Jewish home is never allowed to become a sheer
billeting headquarters for monotonous sleeping, waking,
working, resting, eating and drinking as one goes through
the cycles of living from birth to death. The Torah sets the
stamp of sanctity on every normal manifestation of life. It
dramatizes and blesses the routine of physical existence. The
example of the Sabbath may well illustrate this. It is not
often enough realized that the Fourth Commandment of
Sabbath rest is also a command calling for and sanctifying
work—"Six days shall you labor" (Exodus 20:9). The rabbis

say that he who does not train his child for a trade or other
honorable occupation is as though he raised him to be a
robber. One needs to work to get the best out of oneself and
out of life. This Fourth Commandment after recognizing
this goes on to say, "but on the seventh day, a Sabbath to the
Lord your God, you shall not do any work, neither you, nor
your son, nor your daughter, nor your manservant, nor
your maidservant, nor your cattle, nor your stranger within
your gates (Exodus 20:10). The Sabbath rest must be for all
in the household, children, servants, strangers, and even for
the cattle. This is a repeated theme in Jewish law (Exodus
23:12)—"Six days you shall do your work, but on the seventh
day you shall rest, that your ox and your ass may have rest,
and the son of your handmaid and your alien may be re-
freshed." The Sabbath is not a privileged luxury for the
wealthy; it is a blessing for labor as well as for capital. It is
not for the Jew alone; it is to be shared by all.

Jewish tradition has conscientiously sought to define what
activities are permitted on the Sabbath. Thus, writing or
cooking which are associated with workaday experience are
forbidden. Ploughing, reaping, grinding, kneading, spinning,
weaving, sewing, building, hammering, carrying, riding, mar-
keting, selling, carpentry, and many similar activities even
when done for amusement or as a hobby are prohibited. The
effect of these restrictions has been to concentrate the experience of the Sabbath in the home and the synagogue, and
hold it there away from the highways, the golf links, and
public restaurants.

Many are the suggestions for beautifying the home for the
Sabbath. If during the week one comes across some special
delicacy in the market, he should purchase it and bring it
home to be kept for adding to the Sabbath delight. The
Jewish housewife devotes herself on Friday to preparations
for the Sabbath and to give the home its maximum radiance

The Sabbath does not creep in unnoticed at midnight; it begins with sunset on Friday. It is welcomed as Israel's bride in the synagogue and in the home. The family gathers around the festive table. On it glisten the whitest of covers and the brightest of silver, and the shining Sabbath candles which have been kindled and blessed by the mother of the household before sunset. Father returning from the synagogue blesses his children and chants the paean of the true wife that closes the Book of Proverbs (31:10–31). "She opens her mouth with wisdom, and the law of love is on her tongue. She looks well to the ways of her household. . . . Her children rise up and call her blessed, and her husband praises her: 'Many daughters do well, but thou excellest them all ' "

The Sabbath is then formally welcomed in blessing over a cup of the sweet wine that "cheers the heart of man," and over the bread which "strengthens the heart of man" (Psalm 104:15). All over the world special dishes are associated with the Sabbath meal. That meal becomes a communion of family and friends in a joyous religious spirit. The happy singing of Psalms and other hymns of Sabbath joy, and the chanting of the Grace after Meals do indeed transform the table into an altar.

This Sabbath gathering of the family is today the more to be prized as the increase in popular mobility and in the pressures of life tend more and more to weaken family ties and to draw people away from the home. How far the centripetal power of the Jewish home can meet this challenge is today an open question. In many congregations in the United States the synagogue has tried to counter the problems arising from small apartments, the social distractions of the young and the not infrequent loneliness of the old, by holding a late Friday evening service in addition to the regular service of welcoming the Sabbath at sunset. An informal address, community singing, and a convivial hour together with prayers, attempt to reproduce the old time family spirit of the Jewish home on the Sabbath.

The Jew has ever felt that on the Sabbath angels enter his home to bring their blessing. On it he is enraptured by an oversoul exalting his living. He experiences delight in the Lord, just as Isaiah affirmed (58:13, 14), "If because of the Sabbath you will turn away your foot from doing your business on My holy day and you will call the Sabbath a delight and the holy day of the Lord honored, and you will honor it by not following your accustomed way, nor pursuing your business nor speaking of it, then shall you find delight in the Lord." This has consistently been Jewish experience. As wise and philosophic a Roman as Seneca looking on the Sabbath from the outside disdainfully called it a superstition through which Jews lose a seventh of their life in idleness. In truth the Sabbath has ever been the brightest ornament in the life of the Jew. It has given his home beauty of living even in the outward uglinesses imposed by medieval ghettos, just as in ancient Egypt when thick darkness was overhanging the land "all the children of Israel had light in their homes" (Exodus 10:23). The Sabbath validates the dictum of an eminent modern thinker, Ahad Haam, that more than the Jew has kept the Sabbath it is the Sabbath which has kept the Jew.

FIFTEEN

THE JEW AND HIS FELLOW MEN

FUNDAMENTAL to the philosophy of Judaism is the thought that man should strive for personal salvation through the redemption of society. The rabbis say that God Himself acclaims as righteous the one who is good to his fellow men. Our every act affects the whole community. The isolated life of a Robinson Crusoe cannot fulfil a maximal potential of usefulness. We cannot serve ourselves alone. Eventually our family is the whole family of mankind. That is the emphasis of Judaism.

The Torah, be it remembered, was not revealed only to an individual Moses but to the whole people at Mount Sinai. Salvation cannot be self-centered. "Separate not yourself from the community" is a guiding principle of conduct enunciated as a constant refrain by Hillel, the greatest of the rabbis. The Biblical law requires that in every harvest the gleanings, the forgotten sheaf, and that which grows in the corner of the field, must be left for the poor, and in the third year the tithe of the harvest must be given to the landless Levite, the alien, the fatherless, and the widow. Even one who has done all this and can say "I have hearkened to the voice of the Lord my God, I have done according to all Thou hast commanded me," cannot pray for himself alone, and he continues his prayer, "Look forth from Thy holy habitation from heaven and bless Thy people Israel and the land which Thou hast given us" (Deuteronomy 26:15). The righteous prays for the blessing of all. The concept of human worth is compelling in Judaism. There is no division between the classes and the masses. Rank and distinction are accorded to learning. All Jews are called on to election in "a kingdom of priests," and the hierarchy of priesthood disappeared nineteen centuries ago with the destruction of the Temple. The rabbi, a layman, is distinguished from his fellows only by the greater depth of his learning.

Judaism is a religion that cannot be understood or followed apart from its sociological code. It offers no salvation for one's soul by an anchorite or cenobite flight from human contacts. It does not consecrate suffering nor idealize self-immolation. It does not preach willing subjection to want and the glorification of misery. Life must be faced not with defeatist pessimism or escapist asceticism, but with the conviction that it is worth living, that it is good, and that evil can and must be corrected.

Personal salvation not related to the social good negates the fundamental goal which is that of achieving not the sainthood of elected individuals but a saintly world commonwealth. Neither subjective mystic emotion nor ecclesiastical forms and ceremonies can be depended on to attain this end. Social justice must become a reality through sociological functions, such as just and equitable relations between capital and labor, between master and servant, citizen and alien, rich and poor. One cannot read the Bible without realizing how intrinsic these are to basic Judaism. Modern society is in large measure transferring these responsibilities to secular instruments and agencies of government. But they must not be allowed to become remote and impersonal, dissociated from the religious consciousness of the individual. It is well to repeat that the Biblical law (Deuteronomy 24:14, 15) forbids dealing harshly with a hired servant, whether Jew or alien, or holding back the worker's pay beyond sundown. In avowing the human equality of master and servant, Job (31:13–15) declares "I have not despised the cause of my manservant or of my maidservant . . . Did not He who made me in the womb make him? Did not One fashion us in the womb?"

Israel has never been allowed to forget that it is a people of eternal protest against injustice to one's fellow man. The first pronouncement in the Decalogue (Exodus 20:2) is not only a declaration that God exists but that the God who exists is He "who brought you out of the land of Egypt out of the house of bondage." Repeatedly the Bible reminds Israel of their slavery in Egypt as a motivation for their dealing justly with their fellow men. Thus, "If a stranger sojourn with you in your land you shall do him no wrong . . . He shall be to you as a home-born among you and you shall love him as yourself, for you were strangers in the land of Egypt . . . You shall do no unrighteousness in judgment, in meteyard, in weight, or in measure. Just balances, just weights . . . shall you have. I am the Lord your God who brought you out of the land of Egypt" (Leviticus 19:33–36).

In Hebrew the word for justice is *mishpat*. This occurs no less than five hundred and thirteen times in the Bible. Justice is one of the most insistently demanded qualities in Judaism. There is also another word *tsedakah* which occurs one hundred and fifty-seven times. This means righteousness expressed through justice. Over the centuries *tsedakah* has come also to mean charity. It is striking that charity is a synonym for doing the just thing. It is a manifestation of elemental social justice and an essential in human progress. It is not a supplementary quality but a primary basic teaching of the Golden Rule enunciated in Leviticus (19:18), "You shall love your neighbor as yourself." Healthy society demands that the elementary needs of every individual shall be cared for. The Levitical law says (25:35), "If your brother becomes poor . . . you must support him that he may live with you." To turn aside from seeing the poor is to deny human brotherhood.

There is no word in the Hebrew Bible for beggar. The care of the needy is compulsory and not left to the chance of individual goodwill. One may not reap his field to its very border, or gather up the gleanings or the forgotten sheaf, or strip his vineyard bare, or collect the grapes that had been dropped during the harvesting. Like the tithe, these had to be left free for the poor and the alien sojourner (Exodus 23:11, 12; Leviticus 19:9, 10; 23:22; Deuteronomy 14:28, 29, 23:20). One of the rabbis pointed out that when a child is born his little hands are clenched as though he were grasping everything that the world has to give. But when death comes the hands are open wide and empty. It is said in the Mishnah that worthy of Sodom is he who says what is mine is mine, and what is yours is yours. This attitude which rules out all sharing of wealth is the rugged individualism of the jungle. The jubilee year with its cancellation of debts brought even to the improvident poor the hope of a new beginning. Such legislation softened friction and helped establish a sense of social security.

The laws governing Jewish charity are the crystallization in code of what had been general practise. Growing out of the Biblical tithe there developed conventions and regulations which define the amount which every individual is expected to give in charity. The tithe is the standard; less than that is termed niggardly. One may give up to a generous fifth of one's income, but unless one is wealthy he should not donate more lest thereby he reduce himself to need support. The gifts should be proportionate to the needs of the recipient, and it should be given with a glad face and with encouraging words. The obligation of almsgiving rests upon everyone, even upon the poor, and one must give of one's best. Emphasis is placed on the merit of inducing others to give. The measure of merit accorded to giving is set in eight grades, the highest of all being to help the needy help himself to become self-supporting, through giving him a loan, or joining with him in business partnership, or finding him work. The next to the highest grade is that exemplified by the Chamber of the Silent in the Temple of Jerusalem, where the giver did not know who was the recipient, and the recipient was not shamed by knowing from whom he received. The third degree of charity is when the giver knows who is the recipient, but the one who receives the gift does not know who is the giver. The fourth is when the recipient knows whence comes the gift but the giver does not know who receives it. Below this is when one gives before being asked, and the sixth grade is when one gives adequately after being asked. The seventh is when one gives a donation cheerfully but it is insufficient. The gift with the least merit is when one gives grudgingly.

Beyond the call for tsedakah—charity, Judaism also calls for gemiluth hasadim, acts of personal loving generous kindness. The rabbis stress that unlike charity for which one needs worldly possessions, gemiluth hasadim, the dispensing of human kindness, can be done through personal service by poor and rich alike, for the rich and the poor alike, for the living and for the dead alike. This tenet needs to be remembered even in our own day. The state and other public authorities are taking over increasing responsibility for maintaining the aged, the sick, and the unemployed. Nevertheless, there is always the call for acts of gemiluth hasadim: the kindly word, and the friendly helpful deed.

The synagogue has been among Jews the primary teacher of the high principles of social justice and human oneness. It has been the primary center and generator of both tseda-kah and gemiluth hasadim. It has always clearly realized that it cannot create new heavens and a new earth only by the enunciation of ethical and social principles, and by speaking words of solace and encouragement. In the face of human problems and suffering it has not been content with eloquent inactivity and fervent prayer. It has been from the synagogue that there have emanated organizations of loving human brotherhood which have brought help and strength into the lives of the needy and the faltering. In the synagogue there came to birth societies such as those formed for anonymous giving, helping dower poor brides, hospitality to strangers, visiting the sick, and providing education. Strikingly charac-teristic of the synagogue has been its organization of the burial society for care of those who die and giving them honored burial, a highly regarded act of mercy because it is done without the possibility of a reward of gratitude from the one benefited.

Tsedakah and gemiluth hasadim have always taken a prominent part in Jewish life. Moses Maimonides could truthfully say that tsedakah is the mark of the righteous descendants of our father Abraham, for of him God said (Genesis 18:19), "I have known him to the end that he may command his children and his household after him to do tsedakah and justice."

In Biblical days the Psalmist said (37:25), "I have been young, now I am old, but I have not seen the righteous forsaken and his seed begging for bread." This bold assertion repeated thrice daily in the Grace after Meals vividly illus-trates the prevalence of traditional Jewish largesse. Open house hospitality has always characterized the Jewish home. The Passover eve celebration in the home begins with the opening of the door and the announcement "let anyone who is hungry come and eat with us." In the simpler life of medieval days no Jewish stranger arriving on a Friday at a town where there were Jews found himself homeless over the Sabbath. Indeed, there was not infrequently competition in the synagogue after the Sabbath eve service was ended as to who would have the privilege of taking the stranger home. This spirit of concern for the underprivileged extended beyond the individual home and became the concern of the community as a whole. Beautifully characteristic in Jewish life is this sense of moral responsibility for one's fellow. The answer to the insensate and contumacious question of a life-destroying Cain, "Am I my brother's keeper?" (Genesis 4:9) is in Jewish tradition unqualifiably affirmative.

Human equality as an attribute of the state means equal opportunity; human equality in religion means equal responsibility. The rabbis picturesquely illustrate this by saying that if one member of a community does wrong all are affected, even as a whole pile of nuts may topple if one of them is taken. The Torah (Deuteronomy 21:1–9) explicitly demands that if there is found someone slain in the open country and the killer cannot be found, formal expiation of the crime devolves on all the members of the community in which the crime has been committed. There can be no passive onlookers when evil is being done. We are all in one boat, the rabbis say, all are endangered if even one takes an axe to hack a hole through which the waters will rush in, though it be only under his own seat. Society is knit together as one with every action of its every member helping pattern the organic whole.

Jewish teachings evoke a sensitive appreciation of the import of individual action within collective responsibility.

The sense of equality and mutuality in social obligations and functions is fundamental to the concept of human dignity and the religious teachings in Judaism. Two Hebrew terms frequently used express this view. One is *hillul hashem*, "profanation of the name of God." This term is used to characterize any evil action by an individual which brings opprobrium on the community. A wrong done by anyone which casts reproach on the Jewish name is a *hillul hashem*. Complementarily, when an individual Jew does a deed of noble service that becomes known, it is not regarded as something enhancing only his personal reputation; it is looked on as adding honor to the name of the whole Jewish community. Any such action is called a *kiddush hashem*, "a sanctification of the name of God." This phrase *kiddush hashem*, sanctification of the name of God, has been applied especially to martyrdom of those who chose death rather than desertion and abjuration of their faith and their people. Judaism regards every action of an individual as organically and inseparably bound up with the lot of his fellow men and as an integral part of man's accounting with the Divine.

SIXTEEN

RENEWAL IN ZION

THE HARSH and cramping regulations imposed on Jews immured in medieval ghettos never succeeded in imprisoning the Jewish spirit. Remoteness in time from the Jewish commonwealth of old and distance from the Land of Israel did not blur the vision of the new Jerusalem and Zion rebuilt. The aim of reconstituting the Jewish people in its own Promised Land recurs as a constant theme in the historic prayer book. In the Sabbath morning service mention of Zion and of the return to the Promised Land occurs well nigh thirty times, in addition to repeated prayers for the rebuilding of the Temple. Collections for the Holy Land are as characteristic an activity of the synagogue as the responsibilities of local philanthropy.

The cruel autocracy which came to a head in nineteenth-century Russia led to the emigration of two million Jews from the land in the thirty years following the pogroms of 1881 and the May laws of 1882. Those who remained were segregated by truculence in ghettos which were swept from time to time by pogroms. The insensate totalitarian nationalism which took such sanguinary form in twentieth-century

Germany savagely destroyed the gains which emancipation
had brought to Jews in Central and Western Europe in the
nineteenth century. Finally it mercilessly extruded or destroyed millions of them by annihilation in gas chambers.
The checks which many countries have set up against
immigration often imprisoned Jews in lands where they were
living under disabilities and persecution.

In the spring of 1896, Theodor Herzl, profoundly stirred
by the manifestations of anti-Semitism in Western Europe
given by the Dreyfus case in France, and in Eastern Europe
by the sufferings of six million Jews in Russia, conceived and
wrote his epoch-making and prophetic pamphlet, *The Jewish
State*. In this he declared that the one way in which Jews
could solve their problem and save themselves was through
the establishment of the Jewish people in an autonomous
state in Palestine that would be guaranteed by the Great
Powers. He became the founder of the Zionist movement, the
aim of which was "establishing for the Jewish people a publicly recognized and legally secured home in Palestine." For
the poet Byron even within his compassion the Jewish exile
was a final doom. He cried out, "Oh! Weep for those that
wept by Babel's stream, whose shrines are desolate, whose land
a dream . . . The wild dove hath her nest, the fox his cave,
mankind their country, Israel but the grave." For George
Eliot a restored Jewish commonwealth was a dream. For
Herzl it was a reality. After the world Zionist Congress which
he called together in 1897 in Switzerland, he wrote: "At
Basle I founded the Jewish state . . . In another fifty years
everyone will realize it." This prophecy literally came true
when on November 29, 1947, the General Assembly of the
United Nations voted that there be set up a Jewish state in
Palestine.

The gates of hope for the Jewish renascence in the land
of Israel itself had been somewhat eased for opening in the

middle of the nineteenth century by Sir Moses Montefiore. A definite movement of agricultural colonization began around 1870. It received new manpower and ardent ideological enthusiasm from "the Lovers of Zion," a movement which after 1882 brought new courage and hope to stricken Russian Jewry. Then, despite opposition from many quarters, Herzl with his single-minded mission found his way to the heart of fellow Jews whom he inflamed with his realistic vision of Zion rebuilt. Their ardent dedication to the millennial Jewish hope of return to the Promised Land of their fathers was dramatically exemplified some half a century ago. A dazzling offer came from the British government to make available in East Africa in the neighborhood of Uganda a territory for Jewish refugees escaping the inhuman persecution to which they were subjected in Czarist Russia. This magnificent gesture was warmly acclaimed by most Jews; but it was the Russian Jews themselves who rejected this territorial movement because they felt it to be a deflection from the unitary Jewish focus on the Promised Land.

The political preface to the reality of the Jewish state was written in 1917 in England when Arthur James Balfour representing the government of that country issued the Balfour Declaration. This proclaimed to the world that "His Majesty's Government view with favor the establishment in Palestine of a national home for the Jewish people, and will use their best endeavors to facilitate the achievement of this object, it being clearly understood that nothing shall be done which may prejudice the civil and religious rights of existing non-Jewish communities in Palestine, or the rights and political status enjoyed by Jews in any other country." Only a few days later the opening up of the ancient land to its Jewish children was dramatically symbolized during the First World War. December 9, 1917, was the first day of Hanukkah, the festival of the rescue of the Jewish homeland

by the Maccabees of old. On that very day, the British com-
mander, General Allenby, entered Jerusalem with his victorious forces. Among them were many soldiers in the three
battalions of the Royal Fusiliers who made up the Jewish
legion organized by Vladimir Jabotinsky. They had volun-
teered as modern Maccabees to help reclaim their Promised
Land. Allenby paid eloquent tribute to his Jewish soldiers
and to the help given him by such men as Aaron Aaronson,
agriculturist, pioneer, strategist.

The Jewish pioneers of the new settlement in the ancient
homeland continued to work intensively to build up the
Promised Land. The many burgeoning settlements, their
dynamic development of the backward and neglected province which Palestine had been, and the inspiration given the
new settlers by the glowing promises of the ancient Hebrew
prophets, all united in laying the foundations for the Jewish
state. The work of Theodor Herzl was continued under the
leadership of Chaim Weizmann, Henrietta Szold, David Ben
Gurion, and others whose names will not be forgotten in
Jewish history.

Within one generation from 1917 to 1947, there was
finally seen the realization of the dream of two thousand
years. Less than half a year after the United Nations had
made their declaration that there should be a Jewish state
in Palestine, in May 1948, the Jews of that land proclaimed
Israel to be an independent state. This newly born State
of Israel was to give all Jews everywhere a new background
of stability, normalcy, self-respect, regeneration, and dignity
among the peoples of the earth. It fulfilled the words spoken
fourteen years earlier by Einstein who saw therein for Jews
everywhere "the self-respect that is necessary to a healthy
existence."

Today Jewry is not an amorphous mass, uneasy victims of
the malice of anti-Semitism. Today, there need no longer be

in the Jewish people masses of homeless wanderers, pathetically craving recognition, status, freedom, shelter, and a home. The State of Israel has opened wide its gates to all who have wished to come to its shores, and to all those piteous victims of persecution who have had to flee lands of Europe, Asia, and Africa, in which their ancestors had lived for many centuries, and who all too often found the doors closed before them in so many other lands.

In its Declaration of Independence the newly born State of Israel declared, "The land of Israel was the birthplace of the Jewish people. Here their spiritual, religious and national identity was formed. Here they achieved independence and created a culture of national and universal significance. Here they wrote and gave the Bible to the world." Israel, the Declaration of Independence went on to say, "will promote the development of the country for the benefit of all its inhabitants; will be based on precepts of liberty, justice and peace taught by the Hebrew prophets; will uphold the full social and political equality of all its citizens without distinction of race, creed or sex; will guarantee full freedom of conscience, worship, education and culture; will safeguard the sanctity and inviolability of shrines and holy places of all religions; and will dedicate itself to the principles of the Charter of the United Nations."

Occasionally one hears of protestations from the individuals who seem to think in terms of narrowly monolithic culture, and who disavow the undying love of Zion which has moved the Jew for twenty-five hundred years since by the waters of Babylon he said (Psalm 137:5), "If I forget thee, O Jerusalem, may my right hand fail." They ignore repeated statements from United States leaders such as Supreme Court Justice Louis D. Brandeis who declared, "Let no American imagine that Zionism is inconsistent with patriotism . . . Every Irish American who contributed towards advancing home rule was a better man and a better American for the sacrifice he made. Every American Jew who aids in the advancing of the Jewish settlement in Palestine, though he feels that neither he nor his descendants will ever live there, will likewise be a better Jew and a better American for doing so . . . Indeed, loyalty to America demands rather that each American Jew become a Zionist. For only through the ennobling effort of its strivings can we develop the best that is in us and give to this country the full benefit of our great inheritance." Any presumption of conflict between loyalty as a citizen and devotion to the Zionist cause is based on a complete misunderstanding of Judaism, of Zionism, of history, and of the character of one's country. To the millions of Jews who have both prayed and labored for the rebirth of Zion, and I am proud to have been since my youth among them, modern Zionism and Israel reborn have added immeasurably to what it means to be a Jew.

SEVENTEEN

JUDAISM AND UNIVERSALISM

THE BIBLE opens with a universal conception of creation. God is Father of all mankind. Ha-Adam, the first man, was the progenitor of all men. The corollary is inescapable—all men are brothers.

The Talmud tells in a deeply significant legend that when God was about to create man He gathered dust from the four corners of the earth, and it was from that dust that man was created. Thus no land can boast of being man's birthplace. This is as broad as the earth itself. Humanity is one because God is one. Moreover, because we are all descended from one common ancestor, no denizen of this earth may claim superior origin to any other. From these religious traditions the rabbis drew the pointed lessons that to destroy an individual life is as though one destroyed the whole world, and to preserve the life of any fellow man is as though one had preserved the whole world.

The Hebrew patriarchs, Abraham, Isaac and Jacob, looked to a God of righteousness and justice at a time when Ishtar and Zeus, Mithra, Moloch and Osiris, and other man-made amoral gods emphasized conflicts among peoples. God, "the

God of the spirits of all flesh" (Numbers 16:22, 27:16), "in whose hand is the soul of every living thing and the breath of all men" (Job 12:10) could not be a dividing deity. The Bible depicts a new beginning after the great flood. With Noah all mankind was literally in the same boat. Shem, eponymous ancestor of the peoples of Asia, Ham of Africa, and Japhet of Europe, are brothers, sons of the righteous man who lived in God's grace. Their descendants therefore are brother peoples, all offspring of the same earthly progenitors. When Abraham was told of the coming destruction of Sodom and Gomorrah, he did not think of their people as alien to himself, infamously wicked though they were. He pleaded fervently and repeatedly, that all might be saved for the sake of the righteous among them (Genesis 19). One of the rabbis of eighteen centuries ago, Ben Azzai, when asked what was the most significant verse in the whole Bible pointed to the opening of the fifth chapter of Genesis, "This is the book of the generations of man. In the day that God created man, in the image of God He created him." His contemporary, Rabbi Akiba, also declared that man is beloved in that he is created in the image of God; but greater yet is the love that revealed this in the words, "in the image of God He made him" (Genesis 1:27).

The oneness of all mankind is basic in Jewish thinking. The Psalmist (145:9, 18) sees God as "good to all and His tenderness . . . over all His works," and "the Lord is nigh to all who call upon Him, to all who call upon Him in truth." For one who truly believes that there is but one God there can be no paltering with race prejudices, whether primitively expressed or masquerading as pseudoscience. The concept of humanity was born with the realization of the universal God. The ancient Egyptians scorned and despised men of other race. The ancient Greeks divided humanity into two classes—Greeks and barbarians. The Jew within his deep religious sense of election strove to look upon the alien, the non-Jew, without yielding to man's all too common facile contempt of the stranger. For his prophets had taught him that there must be one humanity of brothers since there is one Deity and "the God of the whole earth He shall be called" (Isaiah 54:5).

In the days of Isaiah the two nations from whom the Jewish people suffered most bitterly were Egypt and Assyria. Yet the prophet sublimely sees that the day will come when "Israel shall be the third with Egypt and Assyria a blessing in the midst of the earth, that the Lord of hosts has blessed him saying, 'Blessed be Egypt My people, Assyria the work of My hands, and Israel My inheritance' " (Isaiah 19:24, 25). In the twentieth century, in our day, General Smuts stated that the League of Nations was the vision first of all of a great Jew . . . the prophet Isaiah. At the gateway of the United Nations building words of the same prophet are inscribed (Isaiah 2:4), "They shall beat their swords into plowshares and their spears into pruning-hooks; nation shall not lift up sword against nation, neither shall they learn war any more."

The Bible reveals God as visiting transgressions not only on Judah and Israel, but also on Syria, the Philistines, Phoenicia, Edom, Ammon, Moab, Egypt, and Assyria. All peoples equally are bound by the moral law. As the story of Jonah tells, the one universal God was as concerned with the evil and the good in Nineveh, the great heathen city of Assyria, as he was with Jerusalem, the holy city of Israel. Multiplicity of gods led to multiple standards of morality. A god would take under his protection his own adherents. Homer depicts the Greek gods as arbitrarily interfering in the combat of earthly warriors, each god or goddess showing partiality to his or her favorite hero. Israel has no privileged position under God, and the prophet Amos (9:7) declares that before Him the children of Israel are as the children of the Ethiopians. He brought up Israel from the land of Egypt; but He also brought the Philistines from Kaftor and the Syrians from Kir. When the Jew declares "Hear, O Israel, the Lord is *our* God", he completes the thought with the words "the Lord is one" (Deuteronomy 6:4).

The concept of basic unity among men was very strong. We find it not only in prophetic visions but also repeatedly in sayings of the rabbis. With God one and man one, the spirit of true religion must also be one. Rabbi Johanan ben Nappaha declared that anyone who denies idolatry can be regarded as a Jew. Another rabbi, Joshua ben Hananyah, affirmed that the righteous of all peoples, Gentile and Jew alike, will share in the bliss of the world to come. Rabbi Meir referring to God's words in Leviticus (18:5) "You shall therefore keep My statutes and My ordinances which if a man do he shall live by them," emphasized that they say "if a *man* do." Truly, said Rabbi Meir, the high priest himself is accounted as not superior to a heathen who has come to devote himself to the laws of the Torah. It is pointed out further that the prophet Isaiah says (26:2), "Open the gates that there may enter a righteous nation that keeps faithfulness," not in order that priests, or Levites or Jews may enter, but any people which strives for the good. In like manner the Psalmist prays (125:4), "Lord, do good to the good, to the upright in their hearts," without any limitation of race or people.

The Jew does not hold that there is no salvation for those outside of his own faith. What is asked of the Gentile is not that he shall find salvation by accepting the numerous laws and commandments laid upon the Jew; what is required of him is that he conform to the seven laws incumbent on all the descendants of Noah, namely the prohibitions of idolatry, profaning the name of God, adultery, the taking of human life, lawlessness, robbery, and eating a limb cut from a living creature. Within that irreducible moral framework the Talmud repeatedly expressed the concept, still a remote reality, of the basic unity of religion itself. In one of his hymns, Solomon ibn Gabirol who lived in the zealous Middle Ages, looked to the one God and said, "Thou art God and all men of creation are Thy servants and worshipers . . . for the intent of all of them alike is to draw near to Thee." Religion may, and indeed does, express itself in different forms, determined by the varying historical experiences and cultural standards of the peoples of the earth. But though religions may be many, since God is one, religion must be one and universal.

The Jew profoundly believes that eventually this outlook will save the world from race prejudice and other inhumanities which have slowed man's upward pilgrimage. Not religion but religions have been discredited by denials of its ideals. It is negated by anti-Semitism, intercreedal warfare, persecution of religious minorities, dissension and hatred among men and peoples, class warfare, and the social confusion of unemployment, misery and hunger coexisting with the abundant wealth of nature and extreme wealth of individuals. The scientific teaching of evolution at first concentrated its attention on the struggle for survival. It then began gropingly to sense that in man's history mutual aid has been an even more powerful force than mutual struggle in ensuring the maintenance and development of the human species. All men must learn this primary lesson of religion for the more effective furthering of the welfare and development of society as a whole.

From its organized beginning following the exodus from Egypt, Judaism sought the salvation of the individual through the establishment of law, justice, and freedom, as the fabric of planned social living. It has given itself to the regeneration of society by its affirmation of the principles of the Torah

of Moses unsurpassed in conception, and as yet largely un-
attained in practise. It has always recognized that the individual does not rise or fall alone. Economic problems, social
unrest, undernourishment, disease, call for world-wide inclu-
sive human consideration, as the United Nations is now
trying to help us realize. The great Victorian scientist,
Huxley, declared that "there is no code of legislation, ancient
or modern, at once so just and so merciful, so tender to the
weak and poor, as the Jewish law." Something of the harvest
had to be left free not only for the Hebrew poor but also for
the alien. Because God "loves the alien" He says to the
Jewish people, "you shall love the alien" (Deuteronomy
10:18, 19; Leviticus 19:34). It is a refrain in that Biblical
code which so stirred Huxley that there must be one law
for native born and alien alike (Exodus 12:49, Leviticus
24:22, Numbers 9:14, 15:15, 16:29). The cities of refuge were
open to all, Hebrew and stranger alike (Numbers 35:15).
There may be no segregation when the Bible declares insistently that the alien, the stranger, may not be wronged
or oppressed. "He shall be to you as the native-born among
you, and you shall love him as yourself" (Exodus 22:20, 23:9;
Leviticus 19:33, 34; Deuteronomy 24:17–21).

Jewish teaching goes yet further even than demanding that
one must love the non-Jewish stranger. Judaism is truly a
religion of love given by the God of love who revealed Himself to Moses as "merciful and gracious, long-suffering, and
abundant in goodness and truth, keeping mercy to the
thousandth generation" (Exodus 34:6, 7). In the second
commandment He revealed Himself to all the Jewish people
as the God who though He punishes to the third and fourth
generation, yet "shows lovingkindness to the thousandth
generation" (Exodus 20:5, 6). The religion which this God
of love gave to the Jew asks for loving concern even for one's
enemy. If you find your enemy's ox or his ass straying, you

cannot turn aside; you have to bring it back to him (Exodus 23:4, 5). "You may not rejoice when your enemy falls nor let your heart be glad when he stumbles" (Proverbs 24: 17). "If your enemy be hungry give him bread to eat, and if he be thirsty give him water to drink" (Proverbs 25:21). Twenty centuries ago, the Jewish philosopher Philo summed up this all-embracing teaching when he said "Bestow benefits on your enemy, and there will follow of necessity the end of your enmity." Nowhere in the entire Hebrew Bible or in post-Biblical Jewish teaching is there to be found the maxim, "You shall hate your enemy."

The enslavement of the children of Israel in Egypt is a theme which the Bible never forgets. Yet the Egyptian does not figure as the villainous object of hatred. "You shall not abhor the Egyptian, for you were an alien in his land" (Deuteronomy 23:8). When every year with the Haggadah of Passover the Jew retells to his family the story of the slavery of his ancestors and the providential exodus, there is in the story as told not a word of reviling and no call for revenge. Indeed, when the ten plagues which smote the Egyptians are recalled, as each one is mentioned a drop of the wine of rejoicing is spilled by everyone from his cup symbolizing sympathy and pity felt for the Egyptians in their suffering.

For four thousand years the Jewish people has marched through history bearing indeflectibly the ancestral message of the one loving universal Father who wishes all His children to live together as brothers. It has not been and it still may not be easy in our days to tread that path and be a Jew. But it is excitingly stirring and challenging to carry that past onward into the future.

EIGHTEEN

THE CHOSEN PEOPLE

THE QUESTION may be asked how can one reconcile the universal outlook of Judaism and its basic teaching of human oneness with the concept of the chosen people. Biblical history gives the answer.

In a corrupt generation Noah lived as a righteous man. He was therefore "chosen" by God. Every subsequent election was determined similarly by moral differentiation. This was the consideration when Abraham was chosen, because he would "enjoin on his children and his household after him to keep the way of the Lord to do righteousness and justice" (Genesis 18:19). It was because of this that God said to Abraham (Genesis 17:7), "I will establish My covenant between Me and you and your seed after you throughout their generations." This choice of Abraham, and then of Isaac, and of Jacob was because of their striving after righteousness and justice and therefore through them and their "seed shall all the families of the earth be blessed" (Genesis 12:3, 18:18, 22:18, 26:2–5, 28:14).

At Mount Sinai this choice and this pledge passed from a family or tribe to a people. "Now therefore if you will obey

My voice and keep My covenant, you shall be My own possession from among all peoples, for all the earth is Mine, and you shall be to Me a kingdom of priests and a holy nation" (Exodus 19:5, 6). The children of Israel assembled at Mount Sinai were told in these words that they were chosen to become God's people on the sole and explicit condition that they keep His Torah. Thereby and only thereby would they become and remain a chosen and a holy people. When they replied that they would hearken to and carry out the words of God, then and only then did they become a unique nation with a unique consecrated world purpose, with no special rights but with special duties. The Bible repeats the theme that Israel must strive to be holy and rise above such moral abominations as idolatry, worship of Moloch, child sacrifice, superstition, murder, adultery, theft, false swearing, coveting. Then and only then could Israel be God's people chosen to serve as a kingdom of priests (Leviticus 20:26; Deuteronomy 4:37, 7:6, 10:15, 14:1, 26:16–19, 27:9). When we realize that this was always a conditional choice, we see that the term "the chosen people" could with equal accuracy be "the choosing people," the people that chose to accept this world mission. Israel was transformed from a horde of slaves into "a holy nation." Incidentally here it may well be pointed out that the phrase "the peculiar people" used originally in Tyndale's translation of the Hebrew Bible means the people that would be God's peculium, His personal, individual possession.

The chosen people has consistently felt a sense of divine mission to mankind. "You are my witnesses . . . you shall be called the priests of the Lord, men shall speak of you as ministers of our God . . . My servant . . . I will give you as a light to the nations that My salvation may reach to the ends of the earth" (Isaiah 43:10, 49:6, 61:6).

This consciousness that Israel has been called to be the

light of the world has been the élan vital of the Jewish people over the ages. In one of the Dead Sea Scrolls two thousand years ago a scribe of the Essene brotherhood wrote, "Thou hast made us unto Thee an eternal people, and hast cast our lot in the portion of light that we may evince Thy truth." In the daily morning prayers the declaration is made that "we have been chosen from all other peoples and drawn near to Thy greatness to sing Thy praise and in love proclaim Thy unity."

It is striking not that the Jew regards himself as chosen, but that he recognizes himself as chosen not to be a master but a servant to carry the light and the right to the far ends of the earth. "You, Israel, are My servant, I have chosen you . . . My servant whom I uphold, My chosen in whom My soul delights . . . He shall not fail nor be crushed till he have set the right in the earth" (Isaiah 41:8, 9, 42:1, 3, 4). It was in this spirit that the Jewish prophets carried their message to other peoples. Isaiah spoke not only to his own people but also explicitly to Arabia, Assyria, Babylon, Damascus, Edom, Egypt, Media, Moab, Persia, the Philistines, and Tyre. Of three prophets whose words the Bible has preserved, Obadiah, Jonah, and Nahum, we have no revelation addressed to their own people but only their message to other peoples. The prophet Joel (3:1) hears the word of God proclaiming "I will pour out My spirit on all flesh."

This ardent propagation of faith needs retelling. That Hebrew seers of old sought to bring their message to all the world has been largely forgotten during the long centuries when all Jewish missionary movement was forcibly brought to a standstill. However, even without active missionizing by the Jew, his very existence is a living witness to the uncompromised ethical monotheism which he has given to mankind. Both his past and his brave outlook for the morrow are testimony to his conscious determination to live on and fulfil his destiny. In this there is no national or personal arrogance. He is well reminded by the Bible: "Thy Lord did not set His love upon you or choose you because you were more in number than any other people, for you were the fewest of all peoples" (Deuteronomy 7:7). He knows that God dwells with one "who is of contrite and humble spirit" (Isaiah 57:15). He recalls that the greatest among the chosen, Moses, "was very meek, more than all the men who were on the face of the earth" (Numbers 12:3).

All too graphically we know that he has suffered most. "He was despised and shunned of men, a man of pains and acquainted with grief" (Isaiah 53:3). Between his election and his suffering there seemed always to be a connection. He felt himself to be the suffering servant of humanity. His submission to God was his mission. His path has not been an easy one, and his steadfastness has been tested almost beyond endurance. Many have faltered or dropped out on the way. But the people as a whole has remained unshakable. It may have been said in lighter vein, but it is deeply true, the familiar quip about the chosen people—how odd of God to choose the Jews! It wasn't odd; the Jews chose God.

NINETEEN

AWAITING THE MESSIAH

THE HEBREW word *Mashiah*, Messiah, means anointed. In the earlier Biblical days it is applied to the high-priest and to kings. These are not only Jewish kings, for Cyrus, king of Persia is also spoken of as *Mashiah*, anointed. Later it took on the more specific meaning of Israel's ultimate redeemer from its travail. This Messiah as pictured by the Bible is altogether human. He is not a divine being. Moses Maimonides summed up the general trend of Jewish teaching about the personality of the Messiah with his emphatic statement that one must not let it enter his mind that the Messiah will come performing miracles, changing natural phenomena, or resurrecting the dead. Nor will the eventual Messiah of prophetic vision appear for atonement of sins; that is an obligation which rests inescapably on each individual and on no one else. Messianism is a vision of ideals becoming reality on this earth, not in the life to come. It is not some far off event or visionary Utopia miraculously to be attained. It is an ideal that man is called on to realize in this world.

Nevertheless, mystic conceptions of the Messiah run

through prophecy and liturgy. Folk tradition has made much of this. The prophet Elijah is particularly associated with the coming of the Messiah. Malachi (3:23) looks on Elijah as the forerunner of his advent. Throughout the generations the return of the deathless Elijah has been mystically awaited. On the Passover eve when the family gathers to recount the story of the exodus to freedom, a place and a cup of wine are reserved for Elijah, the harbinger of freedom renewed. A prayer for his speedy coming is especially associated with the closing blessings of the Sabbath day. The coming of both Elijah and the Messiah of the house of David is invoked in the blessings which follow the synagogue reading from the prophets: "Make us joyful through the coming of Thy servant Elijah the prophet, and the rule of Thy Messiah of the house of David. May his early advent gladden our hearts."

The fulfilment of this hope is a constant theme in the liturgy. Thus the Amidah, central in the daily morning, afternoon, and evening prayers, opens with blessing God who will lovingly bring a redeemer to the children of Israel. The worshiper goes on to pray that complete redemption may soon come when there will be sounded on the shofar the summons to freedom. May the banner soon be set up to gather the exiles and bring them together to their own land from the four corners of the earth. There may they live once more under their own free rule, with the throne of David re-established in Zion, and God's presence, His Shechinah, once more dwelling in His Temple. No less than nine times do these Messianic themes recur in the Amidah.

The Messiah looked for by the Jewish people will be the man who will bring them healing redemption and will lead them back to a new life of freedom, peace, and joyous service of their Maker in their Promised Land. In post-Biblical eras there cross the pages of history not a few individuals on whom some, and at times many, looked with unrealistic but mystic hope that at last this redeeming Messiah had come. Because of the failure of all these men to achieve this high purpose they have become known as "false Messiahs." Some few were conscious impostors; but others passionately believed that the Messianic call had come to them, or at least that they were the destined herald or precursor of the Messiah. Some had this greatness thrust upon them by zealous and sometimes fanatical followers, and by apparent political opportunity. Almost all of them came to a tragic end.

The Messianic concept from prophetic times and in rabbinic Judaism to this day has varied with the religious outlook of the individual prophets, seers, and sages. But the two concepts of the Messiah as the redeemer of the Jews and as establishing God's reign among men are inextricably intertwined one with the other. The Messianic era as foreseen in the Bible will not be limited to the saving of the Jewish people. It will usher in the Kingdom of God with its regeneration for all. Men everywhere will lift up their eyes and see the transformation in Zion and hear the word of the Lord from Jerusalem (Isaiah 2:3).

The Messiah as depicted in the Bible is thought of as a descendant of King David. He will be "a shoot out of the stock of Jesse," and "the spirit of the Lord shall rest upon him, the spirit of wisdom and understanding . . . and his delight shall be in reverence for the Lord . . . and the wolf shall dwell with the lamb, and the leopard shall lie down with the kid, and the calf and the young lion and the fatling together, and a little child shall lead them . . . None shall hurt nor destroy in all My holy mountain, for the earth shall be filled with the knowledge of the Lord as the waters cover the sea" (Isaiah 11:1–9).

How and when the Messiah will come and how he will fulfil his mission does not partake of the nature of a set dogma. Nevertheless, Messianic idealism has been an active and unfailingly dynamic influence in lifting the sights of the Jew beyond the harsh workaday world to one reborn in moral progress. The Jewish optimistic faith that there will be a better and a redeemed humanity was always a leitmotif for survival, however seemingly hopeless life may have been made by weakness and religious defection, or on the other hand by insensate persecution. Messianism has been an expression of the spirit of a whole people charged with the responsibility of living as a witness to God and a light to the nations unto the ends of the earth (Isaiah 49:6).

The universal outlook is a categorical imperative for the Biblical prophets. Isaiah and Micah use the selfsame words in describing the time when "many peoples shall go and say, come and let us go up to the mountain of the Lord, to the house of the God of Jacob, that He may teach us of His ways and that we may walk in His paths" (Isaiah 2:3; Micah 4:2). For to Him "every knee shall bow, every tongue shall swear fealty" (Isaiah 45:23), and (Isaiah 66:23) "from one new moon to another and from one Sabbath to another all flesh shall come to worship before Him." The prophet Zephaniah (3:9) foresees the unity of man when even the most distant peoples will speak with one pure language "that they may all call on the name of the Lord to serve Him with one consent," and Habakkuk (2:14) declares that the day will come when "the earth shall be filled with the knowledge of the glory of the Lord as the waters cover the sea." Then, says the prophet Zechariah (14:9), "the Lord shall be king over all the earth, on that day the Lord shall be one and His name one." Zechariah (8:23) prophesies that "in those days ten men from each of the nations of every tongue shall take hold of the robe of a Jew, saying 'let us go with you, for we have heard that God is with you.'" The prophet Joel (3:1, 5) awaits a Messianic era when God's spirit would be poured out on all flesh, "your sons and your daughters shall prophesy, your old men shall dream dreams, your young men shall see visions . . . and it shall come to pass that whosoever shall call upon the name of the Lord shall be delivered." The prophet Malachi (1:11) foresees so wide a fulfilment of God's word that "from the rising of the sun even to its going down My name shall be great among the nations."

There was a time in Jewish history when this consciousness of a mission to the world found expression in active missionary effort. We are told that Jesus who charged the faithful disciples not to go among the Gentiles, said that "salvation is from the Jews." He testified they "compass sea and land to make one proselyte" (John 4:22; Matthew 23:15). At the same time, Philo of Alexandria asserted that the laws of Moses "lead after them and influence all nations, barbarians and Greeks, the inhabitants of continents and islands, the Eastern nations and the Western, Europe and Asia, in short the whole habitable world from one extremity to the other." Wherever Paul and the early Christian apostles went they found converts to Judaism. This purposive Jewish effort to win the souls of men continued until the Roman conquest of Judea. Persecution and eventually prohibition by the Church and by Islam brought Jewish missionary work to a standstill. However, the door has never been closed on conversion, and Judaism accepts adherents who choose to enter the fold when impelled by sincere acceptance of its teachings. The Jew looks forward to the day foretold by the prophet (Isaiah 56:7) when God's Temple "shall be called the house of prayer for all peoples." His Messianic vision of the Golden Age for mankind has not allowed despair to overcome him in all his centuried suffering. This outlook made his survival a purposeful and conscious mission.

Judaism is not a narrow or tribal religion. As early as in the tenth chapter of Genesis the Bible views comprehensively

all the peoples, from Ethiopia to Armenia, from Iran to
Greece. The scriptures reiterate the ultimate significance of
the Jew to be the servant of mankind and a light to the
nations, the harbinger of universal salvation. The prophet
Isaiah (42:1, 6, 7, 49:6, 42:4) heard and spoke God's message
to Israel, "My servant whom I uphold, My chosen in whom
My soul delights. I have put My spirit upon him; he will
bring forth justice to the nations . . . I have set you as a
covenant people, a light to the nations, to open the eyes
that are blind, to bring out the prisoners from the dungeon,
those who sit in darkness from the prison." Thus spoke the
prophets. The Jew must remain a Jew, and, however difficult
may be the task set upon him, he may not be discouraged
until he shall have set the recognition of God everywhere
on earth.

One cannot delineate Hebrew Messianism without mention of the concept of peace which enters into every portrayal
of it and is inseparably bound up with it. The most important prayers in the Jewish liturgy, such as the priestly blessing
(Numbers 6:24–26), the Amidah, and the Kaddish, all close
with a climactic prayer for peace. The Mishnah, which is a
code of law drawn up by the rabbis, culminates with the
words that no greater blessing does God bestow on His people
than peace. It is a striking fact that the name of no military
hero is elevated in Jewish historical celebrations. This is most
pronounced at Hanukkah, a festival called into being by
military victory. In all the ritual and prayers associated with
it there is no mention of the triumphant warrior Judas
Maccabeus, but only of his father Mattathias the priest. Not
a word is said about battles and the prowess of arms. God
is blessed for the deliverance He wrought. David is not
popularly exalted as the conquering hero; he is spoken of
as the sweet singer of the Psalms, and as the ancestor of his
scion the Messiah who will bring peace to the world.

The Messianic days are envisioned as bringing to mankind world peace with world brotherhood. In the early Middle Ages the Gaon Saadiah declared that the Messiah could not yet have come because the world knew no peace. In the year 1263 there was forced on the great rabbi Nahmanides in Barcelona a public disputation as to why the Jews should continue to be themselves and not accept the religion of the majority. This disputation which lasted four days was held in the presence of the king of Aragon. At one point in the argument when taunted as to why he would not grant that the Messiah had already come, Nahmanides boldly turned to the king and exclaimed that if the Messiah had already come why was there no peace? If the Messiah had indeed come, it was for the king and his knights to lay down their arms and follow the paths of peace evermore. In the Biblical definition of the Messianic future the nations "shall beat their swords into ploughshares and their spears into pruning hooks; nation shall not lift up sword against nation neither shall they learn war any more." "None shall hurt and none shall destroy in all My holy mountain, for the earth shall be filled with the knowledge of the Lord as the waters cover the sea" (Isaiah 2:4, 11:9; Micah 4:3). Peace is the climax of the classic priestly blessing (Numbers 6:26), "the Lord lift up His countenance toward you and give you peace."

All the implications that can be drawn from the juxta-position of peace and Messianic perfection are deeply rooted in a clear perception of reality. An appeal or a movement for peace that is not based on more righteous living ends and must end in frustration. Judaism holds that there can be no true and abiding peace without growth in human righteousness. Isaiah said, "as all your children shall be taught of the Lord great shall be the peace of your children." "I will make peace your government when righteousness shall be your magistrates." "For the work of righteousness

shall be peace, and the effect of righteousness serenity and
security for ever" (Isaiah 54:13, 60:17, 32:17). In our day
those Biblical visionaries who coupled righteousness of each
individual with peace for all would be called masters in
social psychology, pragmatists, and political realists. Their
evaluation has been substantiated by millennial experience
still in the burning process.

On the solemn New Year's Day and the Day of Atonement,
the prayer is offered up, "Lord our God, inspire awe of
Thee in all Thy works, veneration for Thee in all Thou hast
created, so that all Thy works may revere Thee, and all who
are created may bow down before Thee. May all Thy
children become one fellowship to do Thy will with perfect
heart." This prayer continues with words repeated thrice
daily throughout the year, "We wait upon Thee that speedily
we may see Thy glorious might establish the world under
Thy rule omnipotent, and all the children of flesh shall
invoke Thy name, and all earth's wicked shall be turned
to Thee. May all earth's dwellers understand and perceive
that to Thee every knee must bend, every tongue swear fealty.
Before Thee, Lord our God, may all bow down and worship
and give honor to Thy glorious name; may they all accept
the yoke of Thy dominion. Speedily rule Thou over them
evermore, for Thine is dominion, and ever more shalt Thou
reign in glory. And the Lord shall be Ruler over all the
earth."

History recalls that in the year 1131 in the town of Blois
the Jews were put to death at the stake. As the flames licked
upwards, those standing by at the horrible spectacle heard
singing rise above the crackle of the fagots. In the words
of the chronicler, they said, "we hear a song of strange and
compelling beauty, but we know not what it means." What
they heard was the chanting of that prayer that all men
should yet be united in brotherhood under God. Not a cry

for vengeance rose from the lips of the martyrs, but a sublime call for the Messianic day when men would be brothers.

Twenty-five hundred years ago a Biblical prophet looked on the suffering of his people exiled to Babylon as captives of war. Were their pain and sorrow to be purposeless, asked Isaiah? No, he declared, God's chosen people has a mission for the world. Israel will be the suffering servant, and his travail will redeem mankind. Because he bared his soul unto death and made intercession for the transgressors, as men look on him they will say verily it is grief inflicted by us that he is bearing, and sorrows that we have caused that he is carrying. We thought him stricken, smitten, and afflicted by God, but it was by us that he was oppressed. He was submissive, and he opened not his mouth. He was taken from rule and judging (in his own land), and as for his generation who among them considered that for our guilt he was bearing punishment (Isaiah 53:4, 7, 8, 12)!

Deep within the consciousness of the Jew burns the recognition of that unique spiritual destiny. His existence is bound up with the fulfilment of his mission. He is not a lonely individual on an endless road. Why is he a Jew? In order that finally he may meet the Messiah whom the prophets envisioned. This is his future for which he has lived, and for which he bravely wishes to live and to remain a Jew. His Messiah has not yet come and ushered in a new order of society founded on justice and peace. Oppression, injustice, and warfare must yet give way to Messianic universal peace, universal brotherhood, universal justice, and universal love.

TWENTY

IMPACT ON WORLD THOUGHT

TWENTY-ONE centuries ago the Jewish people fought a victorious struggle to keep alight their religion and the knowledge of God the flame of which was threatened with extinction. It was a time when in the kingdom of Syria a corrupted Greek culture was being forcibly imposed on all. All traces of Judaism and Jewish national existence were to be wiped out. Death was the penalty for any Jew found carrying out his religious rites.

A heroic group led by the military genius of Judas Maccabeus vindicated the right to freedom of conscience, and rescued the religion of the living God from destruction by the worst forces in paganism. The Maccabees preserved light and liberty in a world of moral darkness. Had they failed in their struggle, Judaism would have disappeared from among men. Then Christianity and Islam could not have come to birth. The Western world might still be worshiping at the shrines of Jupiter and Venus. With true psychological insight early Christianity counted among the saints of the Church the figure of Judas Maccabeus though he was born some two centuries before the beginning of the Christian era. The light which the Maccabees rekindled in the rescued Temple in Jerusalem was a light that has not failed. Because of their brave stand it did not happen again that "darkness shall cover the earth and thick darkness the peoples" (Isaiah 60:2). The world owes much to the Maccabees.

From the beginning, Jewish history has been marked by courageous differentiation: Abraham's break with idolatry and child sacrifice; Moses in Egypt, defiantly standing out against inhuman cruelty and slavery; Elijah refusing to bend the knee to the immoralities of Baal worship; the refusal of the Maccabees to yield to the specious attractiveness of Greek paganism. It was stands such as these which gave the Jew ever renewed historic meaning for mankind.

The history of the triumphant Maccabean struggle has been preserved in vivid detail in two books, the First Book of Maccabees, an invaluable historical document, and the Second Book of Maccabees, a work originally composed in Greek in Egypt. These two records form part of a collection that is known as the Apocrypha. This group of fourteeen post-Biblical Jewish works has been given such high recognition by some churches that it is included in their canon of the Bible. It includes vivid narratives of Tobit, Judith, and Susannah; and religious thinking has been notably stimulated by the lofty chapters of The Wisdom of Solomon and the sage moral aphorisms of Ben Sirach which are included in the Apocrypha under the title of Ecclesiasticus.

The fundamental indebtedness of Christianity to Judaism is well recognized. The literature of the Dead Sea Scrolls that has recently been discovered sheds added light on the Jewish origins of much of Christian teaching, bringing into focus many heretofore obscure influences on the life of John the Baptist and Jesus. We learn from them much about the religious turmoil and ferment in the Holy Land nineteen centuries ago. We come to know groups like the Essenes,

hitherto only slightly known through the writings of Josephus
and Philo. We come to see closely their daring religious ex-
perimentation in monastic living, celibacy, baptism, and a
complete communal system of living. Their exalted religious
enthusiasm recalls the lyricism of the Psalms of David. We
have come to know their Manual of Discipline which pro-
jects a society impregnated with uncompromising idealism
of living and lofty thinking. The War of the Sons of Light
with the Sons of Darkness reflects an elevating sense of the
power of the Deity to overcome all evil and assure the triumph of right over all destructive forces. It lifts the veil on
a future of man glorious in achieving the purest ethical
and social commonwealth. Against this salient background
of religious urgency and ecstasy we now see men such as John
the Baptist and his desert followers searching for spiritual
expression.

Jesus was a Jew. He lived a Jewish life, and carried out
its ritual observances. "Think not," Jesus said, "that I have
come to abolish the Torah and the prophets . . . Till heaven
and earth pass away not one jot or tittle will pass away from
the Torah until all is accomplished . . . Whoever then
relaxes one of the least of these commandments and teaches
men so, shall be called least in the kingdom of heaven" (Matthew 5:17–19). He himself grew up and lived among the
Pharisees. They were the mass of the Jewish people. The
name means primarily separatists, designating them as separated from the exclusive aristocracy and priests who made
up the main body of the Sadducees. The word Pharisee has
an alternative meaning of interpreters, for the Pharisees
developed and transmitted the oral tradition of commentary
on the Torah. They were an aristocracy not of blood but of
learning. "If anyone should ask them," Josephus wrote in the
first century, "which of the two things they would choose to
part with, their lives or their religious observances, they

would readily prefer to suffer anything whatsoever rather
than a dissolution of their sacred customs."

The Talmud discriminatingly characterizes seven types of
men found among the Pharisees, leading up from the less
worthy such as the ostentatious, the calculating, and the
self-righteous, to the Pharisees motivated by love. The last,
the rabbis say, are the ones beloved by God. In line with
Biblical tradition Jesus also excoriated insincere Pharisees;
but of the pious he said (Matthew 23:23), "the scribes and
the Pharisees sit on Moses' seat; so practise and observe
whatsoever they tell you." He consorted and dined with
them, and it was they who warned him when he was in danger.

The religion practised and taught by Jesus was almost
entirely the Judaism of the Pharisees. It is largely their
classic teachings derived from the Bible which the Sermon
on the Mount emphasizes. He bade the disciples not to swear
"by the earth for it is His footstool, nor by Jerusalem for it
is the city of the great King." He quoted in this from the
prophet Isaiah (66:1), "the heaven is My throne and the
earth is My footstool," and from the Psalms (48:3) which call
Zion "the city of the great King." "Happy are the meek for
they shall inherit the earth," is directly quoted from the
Biblical Book of Psalms, "the meek shall inherit the earth"
(Psalm 37:11). Paralleling lust of the eyes with physical
adultery is a combination of the seventh commandment,
"thou shalt not commit adultery," with the tenth, "thou
shalt not covet thy neighbor's wife." The teaching of turning
the other cheek is given by Isaiah (50:6) as a characteristic of
God's servant: "I gave my back to the smiters and my cheek
to them who plucked off the hair, I hid not my face from
shame and spitting," and by Jeremiah (Lamentations 3:30)
as the gesture of the stricken Jewish people: "Let him give
his cheek to him that smites him." The call to give alms
secretly was embodied in the Chamber for Silent Gifts which

existed in the Temple in Jerusalem in the days of Jesus,
while the bidding to give help and loans to the needy is
derived from numerous passages in the Torah such as Deuteronomy 15:7, 8: "If there be among you a needy man
. . . you shall not harden your heart nor shut your hand
from your needy brother, but you shall surely open your
hand to him and shall surely lend him sufficient for his need
in that which he wants." The call to show love to one's enemy
as we have seen is found repeatedly in the Hebrew Bible:
"Rejoice not when your enemy falls, nor let your heart be
glad when he stumbles. If your enemy be hungry, give him
bread to eat, and if he be thirsty, give him water to drink"
(Proverbs 24:17, 25:21); "Did I rejoice at the destruction of
him who hated me, or exulted when evil found him" (Job
31:29); "If you meet your enemy's ox or his ass going astray,
you shall surely bring it back to him again. If you see the ass
of him who hates you lying under its burden . . . you shall
surely release it with him" (Exodus 23:4, 5). The summing
up "whatsoever you wish that men would do to you, do to
them" is declared by the Sermon on the Mount to be "the
Torah and the prophets."

The Paternoster well illustrates how much of Jewish religious teaching Christianity has absorbed. "Our Father who
art in heaven" is an appellation of God that constantly recurs
in Jewish prayer and that is based on such Biblical passages
as the prayer of King David who addresses God as "our Father"
(I Chronicles 29:10), or Isaiah (64:7), "Now, O Lord, Thou
art our Father," or Deuteronomy (14:1), "You are children of
the Lord your God." The phrases "hallowed be Thy name,
Thy kingdom come, Thy will be done," are a direct quotation
of the opening words of the ancient Jewish prayer the Kaddish, while the prayer for one's daily bread is an echo of
Proverbs (30:8), "Feed me with my allotted bread." And so
throughout that prayer to its closing words, "For Thine is

the Kingdom, the power, and the glory, for ever" recalling
King David's words of praise (I Chronicles 29:11), "Thine,
O Lord is the greatness and the power and the glory. . . ."

Because of the essential Jewishness of nearly all the teachings of Jesus, and because the disciples were Jews, the earliest
churches were synagogues. As late as toward the end of the
fourth century the Christians in Antioch were regular at-
tendants at the synagogue. The church altar is derived from
the Temple in Jerusalem. The liturgy of the Church including the reading from the Bible and the Psalms was modelled
on that of its parent, the synagogue. The oldest chants used
in the historic church are not infrequently derived from or
influenced by those which the early Christians knew and
loved in the synagogue.

The earliest religious approach to Gentiles by the founders
of the Church was through the synagogue. There they found
many, especially women, who were converts from paganism
to Judaism. When, unlike Jesus, Paul broke away from many
of the fundamental beliefs and observances of Judaism, it
became increasingly easy for him and his followers to win
over Gentiles to his less exacting regime of ritual and religious
observance. Fundamental ceremonial elements in the Church
were taken over from Judaism though given a different
emphasis and interpretation. Sunday as the day of rest is an
adaptation of the Jewish Sabbath, just as Easter is of the
Jewish Passover, and the Communion with its memories of
the Last Supper is a derivative of the Passover eve ritual.
Even the baptismal font is an adaptation of the *mikveh*, the
Jewish ritual bath. Early Christian literature springs in large
part from extra-canonical apocalyptic Jewish writings. The
early Christian, Jerome, who settled in Bethlehem, learned
Hebrew from Jews. He translated the Bible into the Latin
Vulgate, which made it readily available to the European
world. It became the official version in the Catholic Church,

thus helping preserve the influence of Judaism throughout
Church history.

Christianity was not the only child of Judaism. Islam, the
religion of Muhammad, which is the religious faith of three
hundred millions in Asia and Africa, is also a child of Judaism. Muhammad could probably neither read nor write,
but he had scribes and other close Jewish associates besides
the Jewish wives he married. It was mainly under Jewish
influences that the vision of Islam entered his soul. He used
not a few Hebrew religious terms, such as *Sakinah* (the
divine presence), *malakut* (the kingdom of heaven), *zakat*
(purity, alms), and the Aramaic-Jewish word *salat* (prayer).
In the beginning of his religious mission he believed and he
claimed that he was the seal of the Biblical prophets. He was
convinced that he was preaching Judaism and fulfilling the
promise of the Bible. It is true that in his untutored way
he knew the Bible only from a fragmentary and confused
oral tradition. Its literary text was unknown to him, and
in his circles historic Biblical facts could become so distorted
that in the Koran he calls Haman the servant of Pharaoh, and
he confuses Miriam the sister of Moses with Mary the mother
of Jesus. Yet from his association with Arabian Jews Muhammad could say to his own people, "my Lord hath directed me
unto the right way, the true faith, the religion of the righteous Abraham, and he was no idolater," and turning to the
Jews he said, "we believe in what hath been revealed unto
us and in that which hath been revealed unto you. Our God
and your God is one."

He called the Jews *Ahl al Kitab*, "the People of the Book,"
but he broke away from them when he could not convince
them that he was the seal of the prophets of their Bible. Then
in revulsion he ceased to use the Hebrew name *Rahman* (the
Merciful) for God and he adopted the Arabic name Allah.
He changed the custom of facing Jerusalem in prayer to that

of facing Mecca. He changed the Sabbath from the Jewish
seventh day of the week to Friday, the day on which he had
seen Jews beginning their Sabbath, and he instituted that
it be observed not as a day of rest but as a day of additional
prayer. He modified the Jewish dietary laws which until
then he had observed. He had adopted the great Jewish
fast, the Day of Atonement, under the name Ashura
(tenth) because the Day of Atonement falls on the tenth of
the Hebrew month of Tishri. This he changed to Ramadan,
a month of fasting from dawn to nightfall.

Yet Muhammad preserved in his religious teachings many
essentials of Judaism which he had come to know. He destroyed the idolatry which had been current among his people,
and he established a transcendant uncompromised monotheism freed from all association with the legendary three
daughters of Allah and jinns and demons. The Moslem
mosque strictly follows the tradition of the synagogue in
admitting no images. Muhammad eradicated the infanticide
which had been practised by the Arabs under the pressure of
poverty. Jewish influences were also very strong in the Moslem institution of daily praying. This he established together
with the obligation of washing for ritual cleanliness, orienta-
tion in prayer, prostration, and spiritual concentration in
the utterance of set orisons. Jewish influence also expressed
itself in such theological insistence as that there may be no
angelic or saintly mediators coming between the individual
and God.

In the Koran one comes across Muhammad's often confused
references to Biblical figures, Adam and Eve, Cain and Abel,
Enoch and Noah. Abraham is mentioned no less than seventy
times and the Jewish traditional story of his smashing his
father's idols recurs. Moses is recalled by name in thirty-four
chapters of the Koran, and the detailed stories about him,
and about Joseph and other Biblical characters reveal how

indebted to Jewish sources was Muhammad for his transformation into the creator of a world religion. Authoritative Moslem law (*hadith*) not infrequently took form under the direct influence of traditional Jewish law, and Moslem ethical standards are often directly drawn from those of Judaism. Jehudah Halevi in the Middle Ages could rightly declare that both Christianity and Islam help bring near the Messianic future which Judaism has set as the ideal for man's attainment.

Turning from the field of religion to that of secular history, we find many Jewish influences as the Middle Ages flowered into the Renaissance. Jews played an important part as a bridge between the Saracenic culture which had achieved a high level at the time and the Europe which was to emerge from the Middle Ages. Jewish cultural contacts were at times even farther reaching. Jews were among the earliest recorded world travelers. Of the Radanite Jews we are told that in the year 847 they traveled from Western Europe to China and back, journeying both by land and sea. Some historians believed that from those distant oriental parts Jewish travelers may have brought products until then unknown in Europe, such as spices, sugar, oranges, and rice. It also appears to be the fact that the West owes to Jewish travelers its knowledge and its adoption of Indian-Arabic arithmetic and numerals.

In other ways, too, Jews served as cultural intermediaries. Because of their wide contacts and ready knowledge of languages they often rendered into European tongues both Arabic writings and Arabic translations of Greek learned works, especially in the field of medicine and mathematics. Furthermore, original Jewish medieval books such as *The Fountain of Life* by Solomon ibn Gabirol, who was known to the medieval scholastic world as Avicebron, or the *Guide to the Perplexed* of Moses Maimonides, exercised a profound influence on the thinking of men like Thomas Aquinas, lead-

ing spirit among scholastic Christian teachers, and Roger
Bacon. It was Roger Bacon who stated that "from the beginning the Hebrews have been very skilful in the knowledge
of astronomy, and all nations have obtained this science as
well as other sciences from them." The awakening medieval
world owed much indeed to their contributions. The astronomical tables used by Columbus were computed by the
Jew Abraham Zacuto, astronomer royal to King Emanuel of
Portugal. The quadrant used by Columbus, by Vasco da
Gama, and all medieval navigators, was invented by Levi ben
Gerson and was in use until the eighteenth century when it
was supplanted by Halley's quadrant.

When the movement for the Reformation took fire under
Martin Luther's impassioned leadership, his knowledge of
the Hebrew Bible was an important factor in his religious
development. In seeking a true understanding of its original
text he was greatly beholden to the interpretations of such
Jewish commentators as Rashi (eleventh century) and David
Kimchi (thirteenth century). In translating it into the vernacular German, he gave to the masses of his people a religious
handbook of incalculable influence. Similarly, the English
Authorized Version issued at the beginning of the seventeenth
century exercised a potent activating influence on English
speaking people, and spelled an important chapter in world
history. The English people became, as the classic historian
John Richard Green states, "the people of a book, and that
book was the Bible."

This comes out with striking clearness in the early history
of the United States. Lecky could correctly write that "It is
at least an historical fact that in the great majority of instances
the early Protestant defenders of civil liberty derived their
political principles chiefly from the Old Testament."

The Pilgrim Fathers thought of themselves as the children
of Israel escaping from Egypt. They spoke of their journey

across the Atlantic Ocean to their new homeland as a crossing of the Red Sea in a new exodus to freedom. The Biblical code of laws which follows the Ten Commandments was drawn on over and over again by them and the early settlers in Puritan New England generally for the regulations which governed life in their settlements. Their varied codes and constitutions gave the divine will as the authority for the laws. In this way the organic union of religion and social and ethical considerations with political forms and institutions, strongly characteristic of Jewish Biblical law, made itself felt in the early organization of Puritan American states of New England.

Lecky vividly said that the Hebraic mortar cemented the foundations of American democracy. In the introduction to his fourteenth century English translation of the Bible Wycliffe had declared the Bible to be "for the government of the people, by the people, and for the people." Those in America who advocated the Revolution found moral and religious support for their stand in the victorious Gideon's refusal to become king or to allow his son to succeed him as king. "The men of Israel said to Gideon, 'Rule over us, you and your son and your son's son also.' Then Gideon said to them, 'I will not rule over you, neither will my son rule over you. The Lord shall rule over you'" (Judges 8:22, 23). Or they would turn to the prophet Samuel's stern condemnation both of the people's desire to set up a king over them and of the institution of monarchy (I Samuel 8). The words on the Liberty Bell are taken from the verse in Leviticus (25:10), "Proclaim Liberty throughout all the Land unto all the Inhabitants Thereof." Before the present seal of the American republic was agreed on, a committee consisting of Franklin, Adams and Jefferson recommended that the seal of the newborn United States should depict Pharaoh as a crowned monarch, sword in hand, seated in his chariot, pursuing the children of Israel, but being overtaken by the waves of the Red Sea while Moses was standing on the far shore in safety. The motto of the seal was to be "Rebellion to tyrants is obedience to God." When the authors of the Declaration of Independence said "that all men . . . are endowed by their Creator with certain unalienable Rights, that among these are Life, Liberty, and the pursuit of Happiness," they were echoing the spirit of the opening of the Ten Commandments which every child learns: "I am the Lord your God who brought you out of the land of Egypt, out of the house of bondage." These words proclaimed that it was the Creator Himself who took His people out of slavery to endow them with life and liberty.

It was Heinrich Heine who pungently said that since the time of the exodus from Egypt freedom has spoken with a Hebrew accent. In the War Between the States, spiritual justification for the stand taken by the North was adduced from Biblical regulations for the control of the evils of slavery and for insistence on the humane treatment of the worker. In the South the Negro would sing with moving fervor such songs of hope as:

> Go down Moses, way down in Egypt's land,
> Tell ole Pharaoh to let My people go.

Equally fervently they sang:

> When Moses and his soldiers
> From Egypt's land did flee,
> His enemies were behind him
> And in front of him the sea.
> God raised the waters like a wall
> And opened up the way;
> And the God that lived in Moses' time
> Is just the same today.

The timeless social principles of the Bible of Moses are still imperatively needed the world over in mankind's con-

tinued struggle against racial discrimination, religous intol-
erance, social injustice, economic enslavement, imperialist
aggression, and similar forms of barbarous denials of human
rights and liberty. Thomas H. Huxley pointed out that
"down to modern times no State has had a constitution in
which the interests of the people are so largely taken into
account, in which the duties so much more than the privileges
of the rulers are insisted upon, as that drawn up for Israel
in Deuteronomy and Leviticus." He characterized it as the
Magna Carta of the poor and the oppressed, and he declared
that throughout the history of the Western world the teachings of the Bible "have been the greatest instigators of revolt
against the worst forms of clerical and political despotism."

Besides the contribution of Judaism to world thought, one
may pause to mention the contribution of some Jewish individuals to world culture. Many are surprised to learn of
the close ties between the discovery of the New World and
Jewish scientists and scholars who were often Marranos, that
is escapees from persecution who were compelled to live as
secret Jews. Many historians are convinced that Christopher
Columbus himself knowingly had such a Jewish background.
Many facts have been adduced in support of this view.
When he was being so often rebuffed, his historic voyage
was made possible by the support given him by Luis de San-
tangel, the royal chancellor, and Gabriel Sanchez, the royal
treasurer, two Jews to whom Columbus made the first report
of his discovery. It has been keenly said that it was not Queen
Isabella's jewels but her Jews who financed his expeditions.
One may also recall that on his epoch-making voyage there
were in his small crew at least five crypto—Jews who had had
to renounce their faith publicly in order to escape death.
These were Bernal, the physician, Marco, the surgeon, Rod-
rigo Sanchez, the first to see land, Alonzo de la Calle, and
Luis de Torres, the interpreter. De Torres was the first sent

ashore in the new land because among the languages which
he knew was Hebrew, and it was thought to be not unlikely
that the strange inhabitants they there found might be the
Hebrew-speaking "lost tribes of Israel" from Biblical days.

In our own day many original thinkers whose field of work
was not necessarily tied up with religious thought and activity
have nevertheless been fundamentally related to the Hebraic
vision and philosophy of old. Ludwig L. Zamenhof, the father
of Esperanto, hoped to bring the world of men together
as one by the use of a common language. David Lubin did
indeed help to bring the nations of the world together
through his plan of an international bureau of information
and cooperation in agricultural production. Henri Bergson
taught that within man was an unextinguishable creative
spark. Sigmund Freud uncovered deeper recesses of human
consciousness. Albert Einstein revealed new vistas of knowledge, all of which helped make manifest the overriding unity
of the universe. Since the days of Moses and Moses Maimonides many Jews have shown creative interest in public health.
In our day, the names of August von Wasserman, Paul
Ehrlich, Waldemar Haffkine, Bela Schick, Selman A. Waks-
man, Jonas Salk, and many others, are written large in
medical history.

Above all we must go back to the Hebrew Bible for a true
evaluation of pioneering Jewish influence on the world.
Translated into all languages it has reached peoples through
their mother tongue and the sharing of deeply felt experiences and aspirations. Thus the Bible became the foundation
of Western civilization. Its spiritual standards, moral values,
optimistic interpretation of life, and its enunciation of democratic and political society based on justice, liberty, equality,
and man's right to happiness, and its ideal of progressive
human uplift for all, will remain the light sought by man's
groping soul.

TWENTY-ONE

TO THINE OWN SELF BE TRUE

WHY AM I A JEW and feel it as a sacred destiny to be one? How has an accident of birth become my choice? Why in the face of all difficulties that it has involved have the Jewish people persisted in their desire to maintain their Jewish selfhood? Why have they hearkened through blood and tears to the behest of the wise master of Proverbs (22:28): "Remove not the ancient landmark which your fathers have set" and made loyalty a signet seal of Judaism?

A thousand years ago the Gaon Saadiah seeing the sufferings of his people said that one who ridicules us because of our faith, and who thinks us fools for enduring so much when we could readily find happiness by leaving the fold, is truly lacking in understanding. He may be compared with a man who had never seen the sowing of precious seeds of grain. Such a man would laugh at someone whom he saw toiling to throw them out over a field, for he would not understand that the harvest would follow, and bring in many times more precious food than that which has been cast out.

The Jew has been called God's experiment with man. It is for him however humbly to help bring in God's harvest on earth. He wills fervently to play his part in the great epic known as Jewish history. Nineteen centuries ago Rabbi Tarfon said that though it is not incumbent on one to finish the work to be done, none is free to evade doing his part. Man cannot live for himself alone.

The Jew takes his place in a great tradition, a tradition not of conquest, subjugation and empire building, but of a compelling charge to share in God's work on earth. By being a Jew one is potentially serving a cause infinitely greater than oneself. Jewish history furnishes the most striking eugenic experiment in human selection. It has been motivated for a hundred generations by a conscious urge towards a specific spiritual norm. The whole of that history is the record of the struggle of a consecrated will to preserve those spiritual values. From the days of Abraham when the choice was made between an Isaac who would bear the heritage and an Ishmael who would not; from the days of Isaac, when Jacob accepted the mission for which Esau was unfit, this unique process of selection has continued. Many faltered and many abandoned their people at all the crossroads of their history. From the days of Moses there have been those who clamored for the fleshpots of Egypt. The loyal remnant of Joshuas and Calebs survived to enter the Promised Land. The handful of Maccabean stalwarts rekindled the pure flame on the altar and assured the survival of Judaism.

Under the onslaught of the fanatical forces of early Islam, the bloody sword of the Crusaders, and the flames of the *autos-da-fe*, countless Jews went down to their death. But among the survivors there were always resolute standard bearers who continued to live as Jews. Among the most inspiringly loyal to their religious traditions were those living in lands most marked by anti-Jewish violence and pogroms. In our own generation we have seen how the unspeakable holocaust perpetrated by Hitler both strengthened the resolve of the loyal and oftimes aroused in the passive Jews greater will to uphold their Judaism. Persecution has caused some peoples to disappear from the face of the earth. Yet I can say with millions of others the firm words of Mattathias (I Maccabees 2:19, 20), "Though all the peoples . . . fall away every one from the religion of their fathers . . . yet will I and my sons and my brethren walk in the covenant of our fathers."

Being a Jew has meant being a member of a people which consciously and willingly chose to accept the Ten Commandments, and which over the ages has been willing if necessary to be the world's martyr people, despised and rejected by men, knowing sorrows and acquainted with grief. As the Jew sees the challenge presented by the dark pages of today, the call becomes all the more compelling for him to serve his fellow men by being true to himself.

In the United States, freedom to be oneself was built up by heroes who dared fight the battle for religious individuality and liberty of conscience. America is the cradle of cultural and religious pluralism. The Pilgrim Fathers, the Huguenot refugees, the Quaker devotees, and others, braved every difficulty and danger to assert their right to religious selfhood. The Jew also has taken his place with dignity in this noble chapter of the American story, and so must he continue to do. The tradition of American democracy and freedom is strengthened and honored by spiritual loyalty, independence, forthright adherence to one's religious, ethical and cultural heritage rather than by the blurring of one's individuality in a monotonous sameness.

The Jew who lacks conscious knowledge of his past and the will for Jewish survival becomes a meaningless deviant from the majority. But the Jew who knows why he is one and why he wishes to remain one stands out as consciously embodying three to four thousand years of faith-finding tradition. It is his unique distinction to be of the people who at the tumultuous shore of the Red Sea plunged forward with new-born aspirations for freedom. He can face the world as one of the people who at Mount Sinai received for all mankind the law of justice, love, and moral grandeur.

He is called on to remain a Jew in order to help maintain these values and teachings for himself and for the world. As one conscious of this God-given mission he has to help preserve a sense of high Jewish purpose. To remain a Jew through unthinking momentum or in obstinate reaction to the pinpricks of anti-Semitism would be unworthy and in large measure unmeaning. There is no special virtue in standing alone where no principle is involved. But where high purpose is sought, one must preserve individuality with its elements of difference from others, however arduously taxing this determined maintenance of selfhood may be. "This above all, to thine own self be true . . ."

For three thousand and more years Jews have achieved the miracle of survival by daring to be true to their heritage and conserving and transmitting the eternal principles of their religion. Judaism has not been only a theological system; it is the whole historical, social, moral and religious culture of the Jewish people, going back to the cosmic religious sense of the founder, Abraham. By heroic loyalty to their Judaism they did not allow this vision to be blotted out by Babylonians, Canaanites, Egyptians, Amorites, Phoenicians, Assyrians, Persians, Syrians, Greeks, Romans, in a world of idolatry. Their loyalty to this unique tradition preserved their spiritual integrity for themselves, and thereby a vision of God for all men. While not a few weakened and were lost on the way, even if at times there was only a saving remnant, the Jewish people preserved and followed this high purpose whatever persecution or martyrdom may have been brought down on them, when but a word of renunciation could have won for them freedom from age-long agony.

History is a continuum; it knows no stopping place. The Jew has to help mold tomorrow by continued loyalty to his ideals inherited from a long yesterday. Neither persecution nor happy freedom has written a colophonic finis to the Jewish story. Judaism is not a song that is sung; it is a continuing symphony which each Jew may either swell with harmony or mar with discord. It is a symphony which echoes forth to the world Judaism's faith in man's possibilities of good and his power of regeneration to a nobler future. The past is a foundation on which Jews have to continue building and developing in loyal keeping with what has been achieved by the master builders of the past. It is that past which compellingly gives us the dedicated purpose to remain a people for the present and the future. *Noblesse oblige.* The past is my heritage, the present my responsibility, the future my challenge as a Jew.

I have to be a Jew in order to try to reenact in my own life what I can of the God-given purpose of my Jewish people. In the measure that I endeavor to carry out the specific observances of my Judaism with their message for today and their contribution to the realization of the ultimate Messianic promise shall I be truly serving my purpose as a Jew.

Through Moses this word came to his people concerning the teachings of their religion: "Keep and practise them, for that will be your wisdom and your understanding in the sight of the peoples" (Deuteronomy 4:6). Only as the Jew preserves his Torah does the Torah preserve the Jew for his fulfilment in the present day and his ultimate world mission. I have to carry on the millennial spiritual tradition that has been entrusted to me so that in my turn I may help make a reality of the ancient word of God (Isaiah 59:21): "My spirit which is upon you, and My words which I have put in your mouth, shall not depart out of your mouth nor out of the mouth of your children, nor out of the mouth of your children's children, henceforth evermore."

The Talmud recalls an incident in the life of a well-known figure, Honi, (Onias), the Rip Van Winkle of the rabbis. One day he chanced to see an aged man planting a slowly growing carob tree. He asked the old man, "Do you expect to gather the fruit from this tree seventy years hence?" The reply was given, "When I came into this world I found and enjoyed fruit from trees which my father and his father had planted long, long ago. Shall I not now plant for those who are to come long after me?"

We have achieved today a fabulous control over stupendous forces of physical matter, and have created streamlined instruments of effortless living with unprecedented mass production of every form of human wealth. Man's brain has gone from triumph to triumph in building machinery of incredible creativeness, in attaining magical new skills, in scientific agriculture, in destroying distance, in moving with supersonic swiftness, and in a thousand ways making possible a hitherto unimagined enrichment, broadening and deepening of living. Yet we look out on our world of today with an almost paralysing sinking of the heart when we see the terrifying inadequacy of the human material into whose hands is entrusted this world of marvelous, potential power and beauty. For at the same time there have been made possible today's and tomorrow's machines for mass annihilation which threaten the ultimate horror of total destructiveness through nuclear fission. Annihilation by war and the terrors of our peace are not the result of any limitations in man's intellectual powers, which Prometheus-like, can storm the very heavens. The climactic crisis is caused by failure in the soul of man. There can be no real happiness and no security for ourselves and our children except in the measure that we are ruled by what men of all denominations call religion. On this there is new and striking unanimity of testimony.

The multiplication of laws by the state cannot of itself purify society, purge away improbity and corruption, make us more law-abiding, more true and more just to our fellow men. Schools and other secular organizations and institutions must needs fail to bring guidance and salvation to men unless the teachings of religion educate the moral will. Scientific knowledge can lead man to more hideously destructive wars and catastrophic weakening of our fiber, unless Biblical ideals of morality, large-visioned social brotherhood, and human love strengthen our souls and teach us control of the power which technical achievement is placing in our hands.

In the confusion, crisis and chaos of our days, some have desperately sought to find formulas, principles, and affirmations other than religion to save mankind from what may be imminent self-destruction. All too soon it is discovered that neither political formulae, nor forms of democracy, nor the technical organization of United Nations and world government, can rise higher than the soul of the people who constitute them. Mankind's welfare demands a religious transformation of the individual men and women who make up peoples and nations.

Economists and social thinkers have attempted to analyze the racial antagonisms, the crippling strikes, the class strife, and the economic nationalisms that are shaking our world to its foundations. They tell us that we can never have security so long as the power groups of nations and those within nations are moved by a conscienceless greedy self-interest without regard to the rights and the welfare of others. They also declare that ultimately legislative enactments or solemn covenants can never assure social peace and a just economic order so long as men are unworthy. When the social order is endangered there is needed the active constructive collaboration of all. When the hull of a ship is pierced, the traditional cry is not just for the captain and the officers, but for all hands to the pumps. When flood threatens the fields and villages at a river's bank, the call is not just for an engineer, but for every available man, woman, and even child, to build up the levee in fevered race with the torrent. When wind driven flames roar toward the forest, every able-bodied person is summoned to help the firewardens check the fury of the onrush. Each individual must feel within himself a sense of importance in the complex of united action for protection against evil and for the creation of a better life. Mankind can have an assurance of peaceful cooperative living in brotherhood only through a widespread and popular rebirth of social justice. Such passionate stirring of social conscience can arise only out of a more general religious recognition of moral law and the basic teaching of love of neighbor.

Practical men of affairs as well as realistic philosophers have looked upon the supreme challenge of war. From all too bitter experience in two world wars we know that we cannot find peace through national preparedness for war, international military forces, mutual security conferences, or legal pacts for the renunciation of war. We cannot rely on even the best intentioned and most idealistic political leaders to assure us peace. We can achieve lasting peace only through the religious re-education of the people as a whole. We can find the ultimate hope for a warless world only in a new religious education of the soul of men everywhere.

Today it is not only official spokesmen of synagogue and church who call on men to save human society by living with one another in the spirit of religion. This summons, first sounded by the prophets of Israel, is today re-echoed by leading thinkers in colleges, laboratories, and legislatures. They are often men who heretofore have not been notably identified with affairs of faith. Yet in impressive unison more and more of them bid us control amoral intellectualism and anti-social forces among us by religiously inspired social morality lest we go down to imminent chaos and self-destruction. They tell us that technology and the fantastically triumphant machine must be overmastered by the spiritual truths of religion lest human life become a delirious nightmare. They solemnly warn us to control the cult of force by religiously inspired love of neighbor lest man drop calamitously to subhuman standards of existence.

What is called for is something stronger and more vibrant than a tepid ethicism. Nothing less than a new birth of passionate spiritual conviction is needed if mankind is to be saved. The soulless mind is the greatest enemy that twentieth-century man must overcome. Only when fired by religious vision of the possibilities of the spirit can we hope to win the dire battle with evil.

Every morning, seeing man's failures to live up to his best possibilities, we say in our prayers, "What are we? What is our life? What our goodness? What our righteousness? What our helpfulness? What our strength? What our power? . . . Are not the mightiest as naught before Thee, men of renown as if they were not, the wise as if without knowledge, the intelligent as if lacking in understanding? For so much of our days is confusion, and the days of our life are as vanity before Thee." But our prayer does not stop there. We go on, "Yet we are Thy people, children of Thy covenant. We are the children of Abraham who loved Thee, to whom Thou gavest Thy promise on Mount Moriah. We are the seed of Isaac who was bound on the altar. We are the community of Jacob . . . Therefore must we needs give thanks to Thee, praise and glorify Thee, bless and sanctify Thee, and offer song and thanksgiving to Thy great name . . ."

Out of the depths of tested faith and as a commanding voice from ages past, there comes to all men the call to rise above the vanities, confusion and threats of our materialistic society. What of the recurring evidence of repeated moral breakdown, the culminating crisis of our atomic days—"to be or not to be"—the unprecedented challenge to religion, philosophy and science? Judaism compels me to proclaim daily man's greater possibility for good than for evil and his power of self-regeneration. The Golden Age is not a dream of the past. It will be molded out of the ashes of yesterday and the rubble of today. It must be made a reality through our own efforts, our own travail. Here among men on earth we can create the Messianic Age. This is the fundamental philosophy of Judaism. This is religion's challenge and goal.

Armed with faith we can fight soulless knowledge and self-destroying technology; fascist aggression and military violence; racial hatreds, class bitterness and annihilating international strife. We know no better way. We know no other way if we are to build a world in which "none shall hurt, none destroy, . . . for the earth shall be full of the knowledge of the Lord as the waters cover the sea." (Isaiah 11:9)

Why I am a Jew? I have tried to answer why I am, and resolutely will continue to be a Jew.

GLOSSARY

(Unless otherwise stated, the words are Hebrew. Their literal translation is given in italics.)

AB, the fifth month in the Jewish calendar.

AMIDAH—*standing*, the central prayer of the daily ritual, recited while standing.

ASHKENAZIM—*Germans*, in general Jews whose background in medieval and modern times centered in Europe north of the Mediterranean area.

BAR MITZVAH—*son of commandment*, a boy attaining thirteen years of age. Also the ceremony at that age of induction into religious responsibility.

BEN—*son of*.

BETH HAKENESETH—*house of assembly*, the synagogue.

BETH HAMIDRASH—*house of study*.

CABBALAH—*reception, tradition*, mystic Jewish lore.

COHEN—*priest*, a descendant of Aaron, the high priest.

GAON, PLURAL GEONIM—*illustrious*, especially the title of a head of the early medieval rabbinic academies in Babylon.

GEMILUTH HASADIM—*the dispensing of kindnesses*.

HAGGADAH—*narration, recital*, rabbinic teaching complementing the Halakhah. Also the telling in the home on Passover of the redemption from bondage to Pharaoh.

HALAKHAH—*way of going*, Jewish law.

HANUKKAH—*dedication*, the eight-day Maccabean festival of lights.

HASIDIM—*pietists*, followers of the joyous mystic tradition of Hasidism.

HASIDISM—*pietism*, Judaism with the emphases given it by the joyous mystic, Israel Baal Shem Tov.

HAZZAN—*cantor*, the one who leads in chanting the prayers in congregational religious services.

HILLUL HASHEM—*profanation of the Divine name*.

HOSHAANA RABBAH—*the Great Hosanna*, the seventh day of the Tabernacles festival.

KADDISH—*holy* (Aramaic), the ancient prayer marking the end of sections of a congregational service. Recited by mourners as a memorial prayer during the first eleven months and on anniversaries of bereavement.

KARAITES—*scripturalists*, a separatist sect that recognized only its own literal interpretation of the Bible.

KAVVANAH—*intentness, devotion*.

KIDDUSH—*sanctification*, the blessing recited in sanctification of Sabbaths and festivals.

KIDDUSH HASHEM—*sanctification of the Divine name*.

KOL NIDRE—*all vows* (Aramaic), opening words of the formula preceding the religious service on the eve of the Day of Atonement.

KOSHER—*fit, proper*, designating food which is permissible under the Jewish dietary laws.

LEVY—*Levite*, a descendant of Levi, son of Jacob.

LULAB—*palm branch*, used in the ceremonial of Tabernacles.

MARRANO—*secret Jew* (Spanish), one forcibly converted through fear of the Spanish Inquisition who secretly tried to conserve his ancestral faith.

MATZAH, PLURAL MATZOTH—*unleavened bread*, eaten on Passover.

MEZUZAH—*doorpost*, a small parchment scroll inscribed with twenty-two lines of Biblical verses (Deuteronomy 6:4–9; 11:13–21) that is attached to the doorpost.

MIKVEH—*ritual bath*.

MINYAN—*number,* the quorum of ten Jewish men over the age of thirteen required for the conduct of a congregational religious service.

MISHNAH—*repetition,* the authoritative code of Jewish oral law compiled around the year 200.

OMER—*sheaf,* the seven weeks counted between Passover and Pentecost.

PESAH—*Passover.*

PURIM—*lots,* the festival celebrating the story told in the Book of Esther.

RABBI—*my teacher,* a qualified authority in Torah learning.

ROSH HASHANAH—*head of the year,* the Jewish New Year which occurs in the fall.

ROSH HODESH—*head of the month,* the opening day of the month.

SEFER TORAH—*book of the Torah.*

SHABUOTH—*weeks,* Pentecost, festival of the first-fruits and of the giving of the Ten Commandments.

SHAMMASH—*sexton,* the officer responsible for the care of the synagogue.

SHECHINAH—*Divine presence.*

SHEMA—*hear,* the opening word of the basic declaration of God's oneness, Deuteronomy 6:4.

SHEOL—*the nether world of the grave.*

SHOFAR—*ram's horn,* used for clarion calling.

SHOHET—*ritual slaughterer* of animals and birds permitted for food.

SHULHAN ARUKH—*set table,* the code of Jewish law compiled by Joseph Caro of Safed in the middle of the sixteenth century.

SIMHATH TORAH—*rejoicing in the Torah,* the festival immediately following Sukkoth.

SUKKAH—*booth,* temporary dwelling for the festival of Tabernacles.

SUKKOTH—*booths,* Tabernacles, the autumn harvest thanksgiving festival.

TALLETH—*mantle,* the prayer-shawl worn by men at morning prayers.

TALMUD—*study*, the authoritative compendium of rabbinic teachings compiled around the year 500.

TEFILLIN—*phylacteries*.

TORAH—*teaching, instruction*, primarily the Five Books of Moses, and by extension a name applied to all Jewish teaching.

TSEDAKAH—*righteousness, justice, charity*.

TSITSITH—*fringe*, attached to the four corners of a talleth (Numbers 15:37–41).

YOM KIPPUR—*Day of Atonement*, the climax of the ten days of penitence which open the new year.

INDEX